mel bay presents

Irish Melodies

for Harmonica

by Phil Duncan

CD CONTENTS

1	Avenging And Bright [1:59]	**14**	Lord Inchquin [2:34]
2	Believe Me, If All Those Endearing Young Charms [2:31]	**15**	The Minstrel Boy [2:35]
3	Blind Mary [2:54]	**16**	Planxty George Brabazon [1:56]
4	The Galway Hornpipe [1:56]	**17**	Planxty Irwin [4:07]
5	Gary Owen [1:29]	**18**	The Rose Of Tralee [2:48]
6	The Girl I Left Behind Me [1:12]	**19**	Saddle The Pony [1:36]
7	The Harp That Once Through Tara's Halls [2:09]	**20**	The Sailor's Hornpipe [1:56]
8	I Know Where I'm Going [1:38]	**21**	The Sally Gardens [2:46]
9	I Never Will Marry [1:25]	**22**	Sheebeg Sheemore [2:03]
10	The Irish Washerwoman [1:35]	**23**	Soldier's Joy [1:57]
11	Kathleen Mavourneen [3:16]	**24**	Molly Malone [1:39]
12	The Last Rose Of Summer [1:56]	**25**	Wearing Of The Green [2:24]
13	The Londonderry Air [2:33]		

MEL BAY ®

Visit us on the Web at http://www.melbay.com — E-mail us at email@melbay.com

Contents

Alexander's Hornpipe 106
Avenging And Bright 13

Back Of The Haggard 107
Ballinasloe Fair 78
Banks Of The Nile, The 108
Barney And Katey 14
Barney, O'Neill 37
Behind The Bush In The Garden 38
Believe Me, If All Those
        Endearing Young Charms 15
Bendemeer's Stream 16
Black Rogue, The (Life Is All Checkered) 39
Blackberry Blossom, The 79
Blackthorn Stick, The 80
Blarney Pilgrim, The 40
Blind Billy 41
Blind Mary 142
Bold Deserter, The 138
Boys of Blue Hill (1st Setting), The 109
Boys of Blue Hill (2nd Setting), The 110
Bryne's Hornpipe (Tommy Hills' Favorite) . . . 111

Captain O'Neill 81
Cannaughtmann's Rambles, The 42
Carraroe, The 43
Cherish The Ladies 44
Cronin's Rambles 112
Crowley's Reels 82
Cuckoo's Nest, The 113

Dairy Maid, The 45
Dan McCarthy's Fancy 83
Drops Of Whiskey 46
Drowsy Maggie 114
Dumphy's Hornpipe 115
Druang's Hornpipe 116

Ellis's Jig 47

Father Dollard's Hornpipe 117
Father Tom's Wager 48
First Night In America, The 49
Fisher's Hornpipe 118
Flax In Bloom, The 84
Flowers Of Edinburgh 119
Flowers Of The Flock, The 120
Flowing Bowl, The 85

Galway Hornpipe, The 121
Garden Of Daisies, The 140
Gary Owen 50
George White's Favorite 86
Girl I Left Behind Me, The 87
Go Where Glory Waits Thee 17
Gold Ring, The 51
Green Groves Of Erin 88
Green Meadow, The 89
Green Sleeves 52
Greencastle, The 122
Grey Daylight, The 90
Gudgeon Of Maurice's Car, The 53

Harvest Home, The 123
Haste To The Wedding 54
Harp That Once Through Tara's 18
Highway To Dublin, The 55
Hornless Cow, The 91
Humors Of Whiskey, The 56

I know Where I'm Going 19
I Never Will Marry 20
I'll Neither Spin Nor Weave 57
Irish Washerwoman, The 58

Jennie's Chickens 59
Jenny Picking Cockles 92
Julia's Wedding . . . . , 124

Kathleen Mavourneen 22
Katie's Fancy 60
Kildare Fancy, The 125
Killarney 21

Last Rose Of Summer, The 24
Light And Airy 61
Liverpool Hornpipe, The 128
Lodge Road, The 139
Londonderry Air, The 26
Londonderry Hornpipe, The 126
Lord Inchquin 144

Malowney's Wife 62
Mason's Apron 93
Merry Blacksmith, The 94
Merry Harriers, The 95
Minstrel Boy, The 25
Miss McLeod's Reel 96
Miss Murphy 143
Molly Malone (Cockles and Mussels) 28
Molly McCarthy 97
Mountain Road, The 98
Murphy's Hornpipe 129
My Darling Asleep 63

O'Carolan's Concerto 146
Off To California 130
O'Gallagher's Frolics 64

Paddy Whack 65
Paddy Works On The Railroad 29
Padraic O'Keeffe's 66
Pet Of The Pipers 67
Pigeon On The Gate, The 99
Planxty Denis O'Conor 148
Planxty George Brabazon 149
Planxty Irwin (6/8 Time) 150
Planxty Irwin (Waltz Time) 151
Pleasures Of Hope, The 131
Priest And His Boots, The 68

Rathawaun 69
Redhaired Boy, The 132
Rickett's Hornpipe 133
Rocky Road To Dublin, The 70
Rose Of Tralee, The 30

Saddle The Pony 71
Sailor's Hornpipe (Original) 134
Sailor's Hornpipe, The (Pop Version) 135
Sally Gardens, The 31
Sheebeg Sheemore (Waltz Time) 152
Ships Are Sailing 100
Shule Aroon (Come, Oh Love) 32
Smash The Windows 72
Soldier Joy 136
Spanish Lady, The 101
Stack Of Barley, The 137
Swallowtail Jig, The 73
Swallow's Tail, The 102
Sweet Biddy Daly 74
Swinging On A Gate 103

Ten Penny Bit, The 75
Ten Penny Money 76
There Is A Gentle Gleam 33
Tobin's Favorite 77

Wearing Of The Green 34
Westering Home 36
Wexford Lasses, The 104
Wind That Shakes The Barley, The 105

Section Index

BALLADS, AIRS, FOLKSONGS

Avenging And Bright 13
Barney And Katey 14
Believe Me, If All Those Endearing
    Young Charms 15
Bendemeer's Stream 16
Go Where Glory Waits Thee 17
Harp That Once Through Tara's Halls,The 18
I know Where I'm Going 19
I Never Will Marry 20
Kathleen Mavourneen 22
Killarney 21
Last Rose Of Summer, The 24
Londonderry Air, The 26
Minstrel Boy, The 25
Molly Malone (Cockles and Mussels) 28
Paddy Works On The Railroad 29
Rose Of Tralee, The 30
Sally Gardens, The 31
Shule Aroon (Come, Oh Love) 32
There Is A Gentle Gleam 33
Wearing Of The Green 34
Westering Home 36

JIGS

Barney, O'Neill 37
Behind The Bush In The Garden 38
Black Rogue, The (Life Is All Checkered) 39
Blarney Pilgrim, The 40
Blind Billy 41
Cannaughtmann's Rambles, The 42
Carraroe, The 43
Cherish The Ladies 44
Dairy Maid, The 45
Drops Of Whiskey 46
Ellis's Jig 47
Father Tom's Wager 48
First Night In America, The 49
Gary Owen 50
Gold Ring, The 51
Green Sleeves 52
Gudgeon Of Maurice's Car, The 53
Haste To The Wedding 54
Highway To Dublin, The 55
Humors Of Whiskey, The 56
I'll Neither Spin Nor Weave 57
Irish Washerwoman, The 58
Jennie's Chickens (REEL) 59
Katie's Fancy 60
Light And Airy 61
Malowney's Wife 62
My Darling Asleep 63
O'Gallagher's Frolics 64
Paddy Whack 65
Padraic O'Keeffe's 66
Pet Of The Pipers 67
Priest And His Boots, The 68
Rathawaun 69
Rocky Road To Dublin, The 70
Saddle The Pony 71
Smash The Windows 72
Swallowtail Jig, The 73
Sweet Biddy Daly 74
Ten Penny Bit, The 75
Ten Penny Money 76
Tobin's Favorite 77

REELS

Ballinasloe Fair 78
Blackberry Blossom, The 79
Blackthorn Stick, The 80
Captain O'Neill 81

Crowley's Reels 82
Dan Mc Carthy's Fancy 83
Flax In Bloom, The 84
Flowing Bowl, The 85
George White's Favorite 86
Girl I Left Behind Me, The 87
Green Groves Of Erin 88
Green Meadow, The 89
Grey Daylight, The 90
Hornless Cow, The 91
Jenny Picking Cockles 92
Mason's Apron 93
Merry Blacksmith, The 94
Merry Harriers, The 95
Miss McLeod's Reel 96
Molly McCarthy 97
Mountain Road, The 98
Pigeon On The Gate, The 99
Ships Are Sailing 100
Spanish Lady, The 101
Swallow's Tail, The 102
Swinging On A Gate 103
Wexford Lasses, The 104
Wind That Shakes The Barley, The 105

HORNPIPES

Alexander's Hornpipe 106
Back Of The Haggard 107
Banks Of The Nile, The 108
Boys of Blue Hill (1st Setting), The 109
Boys of Blue Hill (2nd Setting), The 110
Bryne's Hornpipe (Tommy Hills' Favorite) . . . 111
Cronin's Rambles 112
Cuckoo's Nest, The 113
Drowsy Maggie 114
Dumphy's Hornpipe 115
Druang's Hornpipe 116
Father Dollard's Hornpipe 117
Fisher's Hornpipe 118
Flowers Of Edinburgh 119
Flowers Of The Flock, The (REEL) 120
Galway Hornpipe, The 121
Greencastle, The 122
Harvest Home, The 123
Julia's Wedding 124
Kildare Fancy, The 125
Liverpool Hornpipe, The 128
Londonderry Hornpipe, The 126
Murphy's Hornpipe 129
Off To California 130
Pleasures Of Hope, The 131
Redhaired Boy, The 132
Rickett's Hornpipe 133
Sailor's Hornpipe (Original) 134
Sailor's Hornpipe, The (Pop Version) 135
Soldier Joy 136
Stack Of Barley, The 137

SET DANCES

Bold Deserter, The 138
Garden Of Daisies, The 140
Lodge Road, The 139

O'CAROLAN

Blind Mary 142
Lord Inchquin 144
Miss Murphy 143
O'Carolan's Concerto 146
Planxty Denis O'Conor 148
Planxty George Brabazon 149
Planxty Irwin (6/8 Time) 150
Planxty Irwin (Waltz Time) 151
Sheebeg Sheemore (Waltz Time) 152

Irish Melodies for Harmonica

Chromatic • Diatonic • Cross-Harp • Tremolo/Octave

BALLADS, AIRS, FOLKSONGS, WALTZES, JIGS, REELS, HORNPIPES,
SET DANCES, O'CAROLAN TUNES

There's something about that Irish Music

The music of Ireland is enjoyed today by musicians and music lovers everywhere. Even with the growth and change of Irish music in last 100 years, something remains that gives the music its distinctive sound. The music was formed in the 18th century. It was used for dance, for entertainment, for making merry, that is, just having fun. Irish music spread to many lands, as well as to America. Over the last 100 years it has become a vital, rich creative tradition in America. *All you have to do to be part of this tradition is to learn the tunes and play them.* The tunes in this book are common tunes that have been performed in the United States for over à 100 years. Playing Irish tunes on the harmonica has been going on for many decades. Most folk musicians are aware that the harmonica is capable of playing Irish tunes note for note.

About this book...

Normally, a harmonica in "C" may be used with this book.

To play the tunes on a higher pitch or key, use a harmonica tuned to:
D-flat, D, E-flat, E, F, F-Sharp or high G.

To play the tunes in a lower pitch or key, use a harmonica tuned to:
B, B-flat, A, A flat or G.

The C chromatic harmonica may be used to play all tunes.

The tremolo and Octave harmonicas can play the diatonic tunes written in "C".

This book uses a Lee Oskar's MelodyMaker in "G", or the Country Tuned Hohner harmonica in "C". (Cross-harp position)

Introduction
"to the player"

This book of 133 selected Irish tunes will give you wonderful music pieces to play on your 10 hole harmonica or double reed (tremolo or octave tuned) harmonica as well as the chromatic harmonica. Much of the Irish music is written in diatonic structure, without sharps and flats. Those Irish tunes that have sharps and flats or extend beyond the range of standard 10 hole harmonica can be played with a touch of the blues technique on Lee Oskar's MelodyMaker and Hohner's Country Tuned instrument. These instruments can play those notes of the melody that in the past could not be played on the standard 10 hole harmonica. The 12 or 16 hole chromatic harmonica may be used with this book.

Phil Duncan

TABLATURE

It is not necessary to read music in order to play the tunes in this book. The arrow and number system notated in this book will get you started right away.

CHROMATIC HARMONICA

Tablature (arrows and numbers) is provided to help you understand the technique in playing these tunes on the **CHROMATIC HARMONICA**. Tablature shows when to blow (arrow up) and draw (arrow down), in which hole (1 through 12) and when to use the button (the circled number). The length of the arrow represents duration of sound.

DIATONIC 10 HOLE HARMONICA

On the **DIATONIC 10 HOLE HARMONICA**, tablature shows when to blow (arrow up) and draw (arrow down), in which hole (1 through 10) and duration with the length of arrow.

CROSS-HARP

On **DIATONIC CROSS-HARP**, the circled numbers ②, ③, ④ & ⑥ mean to "bend" the sound down one-half step, draw. The squared number ③ means to "bend" down a whole step, draw.

The exception is the MelodyMaker by Lee Oskar, hole 3 blow is retuned up a whole step so that you do not have to "bend" hole 3 a whole step down draw, just blow into hole 3 for the same tone. That is why the MelodyMaker is called the no "bend" harmonica. The 3 blow is written in parenthesis (3) every time this note is to be played.

On the changed (retuned) harmonica, the MelodyMaker (G) and Hohner's Country Tuned (C) hole 5, is tuned up a half step to F♯. So that F♯ can be played in draw hole 5. This allows hole 6 blow to be the main or center tone. The MelodyMaker also retunes hole 9 to F♯. With these changes, the harmonica can play most melodies.

DOUBLE REED TREMOLO HARMONICA

The tremolo harmonica produces sound by using two reeds instead of one. *There is never a blow reed and a draw reed in the same pair of holes.* The tremolo effect is produced by a very slight difference in tuning each pair of reeds. In other words each reed is slightly out of pitch with its pair. The two pitches then vibrate creating an "accordion" or chorus sound.

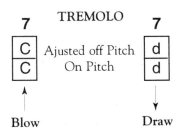

The 40 reed, 20 hole tremolo and octave harmonica is suitable for most playing purposes. *The tablature in this book, arrows and numbers, work for the tremolo and octave since this harmonica is also diatonic.* The tremolo and octave harmonicas are excellent solo instruments. Generally, the double reed tremolo harmonica is played like the 10 hole standard diatonic harmonica.

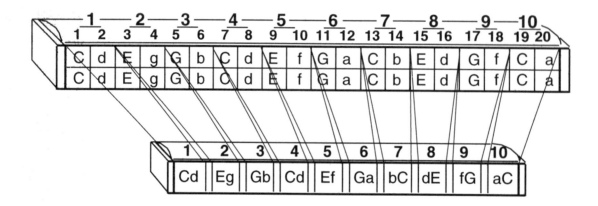

At first, producing a single tone seems easier than the 10 hole harmonica. That's because you don't have to be quite as careful with the placement of the lips to play a "single" tone. You actually expose **two** double holes, **two** for blow and **two** for draw. Therefore the area is larger. This gives you more room to play the "single" note.

As shown above, the first tones, holes 1 through 6 are just like the 10 hole standard harmonica. To finish the scale notice on the tremolo or octave harmonica that hole 7 draw is on the right side of blow 7. This completes the scale.

At first, you do not notice this reverse change because your mouth opening moves to hole 7 both blow and draw. However, you may lose draw 7 if you don't move far enough. The amount of movement, going from hole to hole, on the tremolo compared to the 10 hole standard diatonic is different and will take some time to learn this skill.

DOUBLE REED OCTAVE TUNED HARMONICA

The double reed octave tuned is the same as the tremolo harmonica except the top row of tones are an octave lower than the bottom row. The holes are arranged the same as the tremolo. *In this book the numbers and arrows for diatonic will guide your playing just as if you were playing a 10 hole diatonic standard harmonica.*

OCTAVE TUNED

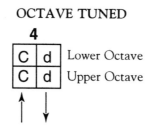

DOUBLE REED TREMOLO HUANG (MUSETTES) HARMONICAS

The exception to all of this is the Musettes, tremolo harmonicas, designed by Cham-ber Huang. This tremolo harmonica plays exactly like a 12 hole solo tuned harmonica. That is, there are double C's at each inner octave. It is a 24 hole double reed, diatonic, solo tuned instrument.

If you play chromatic harmonica, this is a natural. There are no changes. Even the amount of movement is the same on the chromatic harmonica as the "Huang Musettes" tremolo harmonicas.

These tremolo harmonicas come in a case with two tremolos. One is in the key of C and the other is in the key of D flat. Using them both, stacked, you can also play "chromatically". *The tablature for chromatic harmonica would be used for this harmonica.*

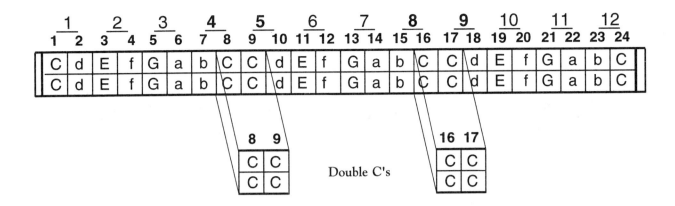

HOW TO PLAY GRACE NOTES, TRIPLETS, ROLLS AND MORE

There are single and double grace notes, triplets, grace triplets and rolls. The use of ornaments is almost entirely up the player and is a primary source for individual expression and creativity. Keep in mind even though ornamentation is part of the basic skill, excessive ornamentation can ruin the intrinsic beauty of the tune. Using ornamentation sparingly is always a good ideal. Also the art of selectively replacing ornamentation with the original notes is equally admirable.

The grace note: A single grace note is a quickly played note inserted before the note to be ornamented. It is almost like making a mistake and quickly correcting it. The rhythm is never interrupted.

Single Grace Note:

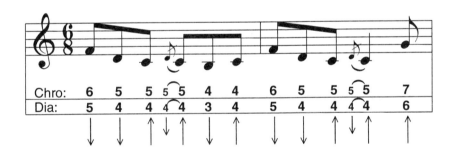

The double grace note: This is two grace notes played quickly inserted before the note to be ornamented. The rhythm is never interrupted.

Double Grace Note:

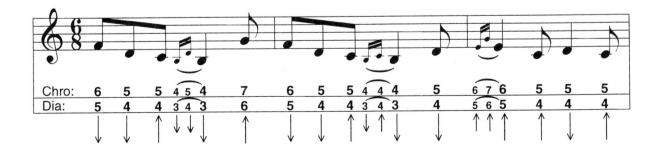

The triplet: The rhythm of a triplet is one count for three notes. By saying the word "tri-pl-et", using three syllables, gives the flow for the playing of the triplet. (Slower 4/4: Tri-pl-et 2 tri-pl-et 4) (Faster cut time: Tri-pl-et an tri-pl-et an)

Triplet:

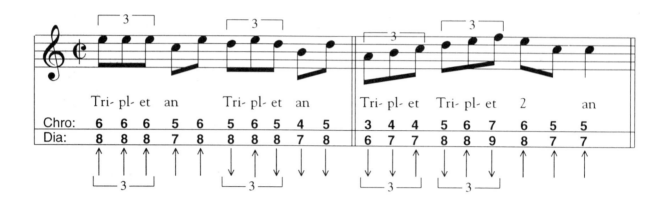

The grace triplet: The grace note is quickly inserted before the triplet, again like making a mistake then correcting it. The execution of this ornament is very rapid. The rhythm is never compromised.

Grace Triplet:

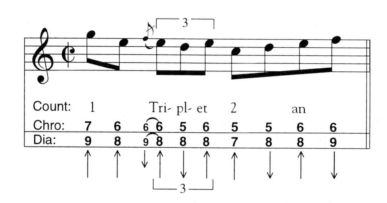

The roll: The roll is usually slurred, slipping from one note to the next, when any of the notes are either all blow or draw. There is nothing wrong with playing the even eighth notes without this ornamentation. Never compromise the rhythm.

Roll:

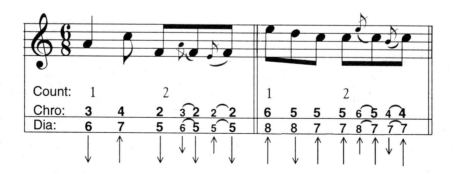

8

Drone notes: These repetitive notes can be played quite accurately on the harmonica. But the amount of practice it takes is phenomenal. Usually the drone notes are left out and the melody line is played in quarter notes. The rhythm must never hesitate.

Drone Notes

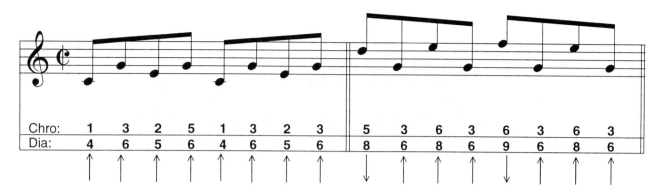

Without Drone Notes

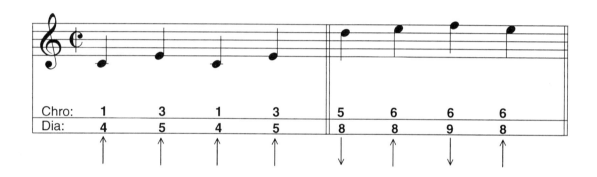

The Reel is continuous eighth notes in cut time, two counts per measure (2/2 Time signature) with an occasional quarter note. The Irish reel often combines eighth notes and triplets. The reel is the fastest type of dance tune with over 200 beats per minute.

The Jig is running eighth notes in 6/8 time with only two accents per measure. This is a perceived skipping type of rhythm, with a very delightful feeling. Jigs are not played as fast as reels, only about 100 beats per minute.

The Hornpipe is played with a swing on eighth notes. The dotted eighth and sixteenth represents this beat pattern. Some players suggest a 12/8 time signature while practicing. It can be played somewhat like the slow rock and roll music in the '50's, but with a more playful feeling. Hornpipes are played slower than reels but faster than jigs.

For a more in-depth study of the chromatic harmonica, *The Complete Chromatic Harmonica* book, video and CD by Phil Duncan are available from Mel Bay Publications, Inc. For 10 hole harmonica: *The Deluxe Harmonica Method* book, video and CD by Phil Duncan. For the double reed tremolo and octave harmonicas: *Tremolo and Octave Harmonica Method* book and CD by Phil Duncan.

CROSS-HARP TECHNIQUES

Key of G on the C harmonica
The C harmonica plays in the key of G. There is **no** F sharp for the Key of G. This works with songs that range from D to E third space.

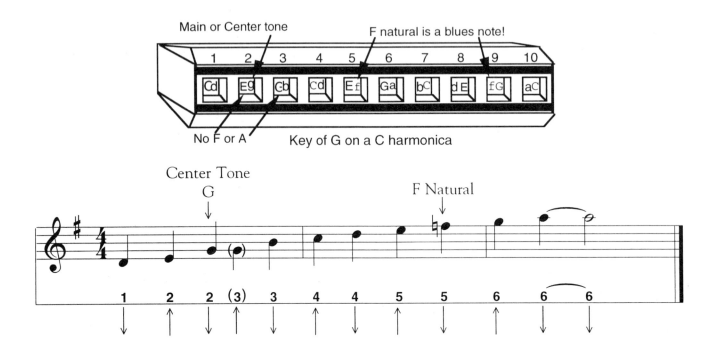

HOHNER'S COUNTRY TUNED

1. This harmonica **only** raises the **hole 5** a half step.
2. You need a Hohner Country-Tuned harmonica in C to play cross harp in G.

    F is raised a half step to F♯. The moves the key "center" to hole six blow.

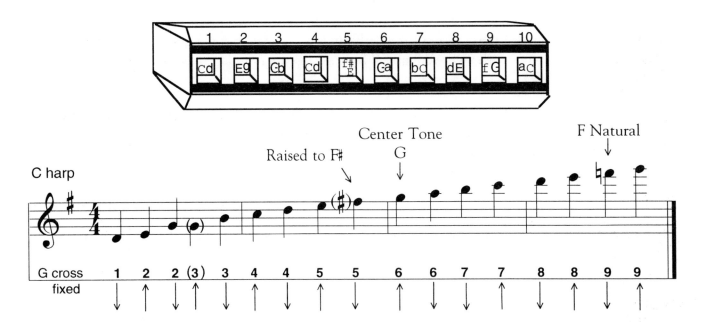

LEE OSKAR'S MELODYMAKER

1. **Holes 5** and **9** are both tuned up a half step.
2. **Hole 3**, blow is tuned up to **"A"**. You do not have to bend draw 3 to get "A".

   Notice!!! The MelodyMaker in **G** is the Key of **G**.

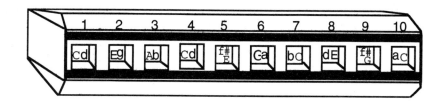

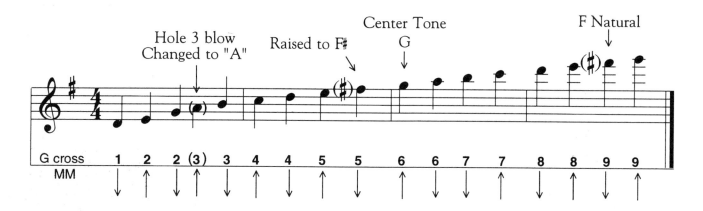

****

For further information on crossharp style: *You Can Teach Yourself Blues Harp* book and video and CD, *Blues Harp for Diatonic and Chromatic Harmonica* book, video and CD, *Power Harp* book and CD, *Easiest Blues Harp book*, *Learn to Play Rock and Blues Harp* video by Phil Duncan.

Rudiments of Music

THE STAFF

Music is written on a STAFF consisting of FIVE LINES and FOUR SPACES. They are numbered as shown:

5th Line ———
4th Line ——— 4th Space
3rd Line ——— 3rd Space
2nd Line ——— 2nd Space
1st Line ——— 1st Space

The lines and spaces are named after letter of the alphabet. The LINES are:

F
D
B
G
E

(Remember the phrase: Every Good Boy Does Fine)

The SPACES:

E
C
A
F

(Remember the word: **FACE**)

| The musical alphabet has seven letters: A B C D E F G |

The STAFF is divided into MEASURES by vertical lines called BARS

BAR   BAR

MEASURE   MEASURE   MEASURE

Double Bars mark the end of a section or strain of music

THE CLEF

This sign is the treble or G clef, because it circles around the G line.

THE NOTE

A note will bear the name of the line or space it occupies on the staff. TONE is a musical sound. PITCH is the height of a tone.

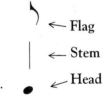

← Flag

← Stem

← Head

TYPES OF NOTES AND RESTS

The type of note (or rest) will indicate the lengh of its sound:

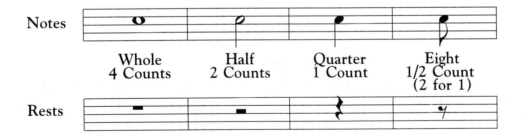

Notes

| Whole
4 Counts | Half
2 Counts | Quarter
1 Count | Eight
1/2 Count
(2 for 1) |

Rests

TIME SIGNATURE

Indicates how many beats and counts in a measure:

Top, number of beats per measure = **4** Four
Botton, type of note receiving one beat= **4** A quarter note

Time Signatures Used in this Book

This 4/4 is also called "common time" and is represented like this:

Cut time
2/2 time
2 counts per measure

Avenging and Bright

Thomas Moore

Barney and Katey

Blow ↑; Draw ↓

Folksong

"Twas a cold win – ter's night and the wind it was
"Ar – ray, jew – el", says he, "Are ye sleep – in' or
"I'll go to me home though the win – ter winds a –

| Chro: | 7 | 7 | 7 | 6 | 7 | 7 | 6 | 7 | 7 | 6 | 6 |
| Dia: | 6 | 6 | 6 | 5 | 6 | 6 | 5 | 6 | 6 | 5 | 5 |

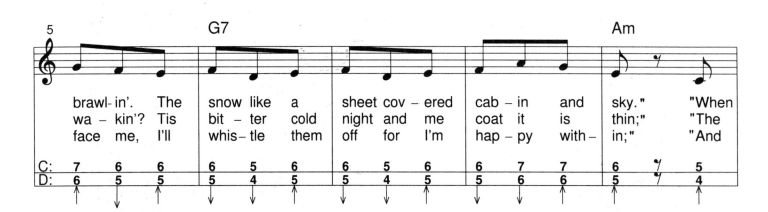

brawl-in'. The snow like a sheet cov – ered cab – in and sky." "When
wa – kin'? Tis bit – ter cold night and me coat it is thin;" "The
face me, I'll whis-tle them off for I'm hap – py with – in;" "And

| C: | 7 | 6 | 6 | 6 | 5 | 6 | 6 | 5 | 6 | 6 | 7 | 7 | 6 | | 5 |
| D: | 6 | 5 | 5 | 5 | 4 | 5 | 5 | 4 | 5 | 5 | 6 | 6 | 5 | | 4 |

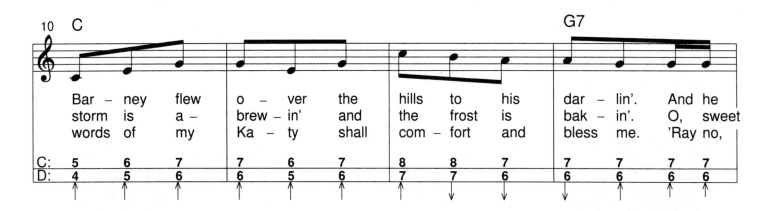

Bar – ney flew o – ver the hills to his dar – lin'. And he
storm is a – brew – in' and the frost is bak – in'. O, sweet
words of my Ka – ty shall com – fort and bless me. 'Ray no,

| C: | 5 | 6 | 7 | 7 | 6 | 7 | 8 | 8 | 7 | 7 | 7 | 7 | 7 |
| D: | 4 | 5 | 6 | 6 | 5 | 6 | 7 | 7 | 6 | 6 | 6 | 6 | 6 |

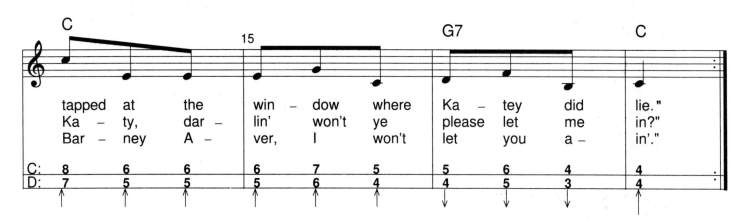

tapped at the win – dow where Ka – tey did lie."
Ka – ty, dar – lin' won't ye please let me in?"
Bar – ney A – ver, I won't let you a – in'."

| C: | 8 | 6 | 6 | 6 | 7 | 5 | 5 | 6 | 4 | 4 |
| D: | 7 | 5 | 5 | 5 | 6 | 4 | 4 | 5 | 3 | 4 |

Believe Me, If All Those Endearing Young Charms

Thomas Moore

Bendemeer's Stream

Thomas Moore

Blow ↑; Draw ↓

Go Where Glory Waits Thee

Thomas Moore

The Harp That Once Through Tara's Halls

Thomas Moore

I Know Where I'm Going

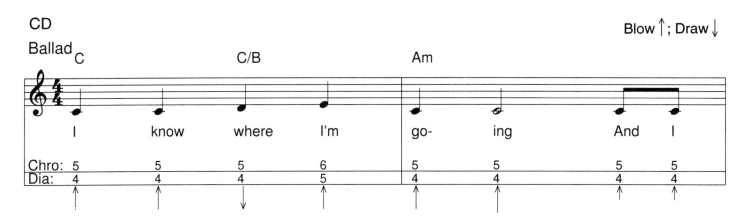

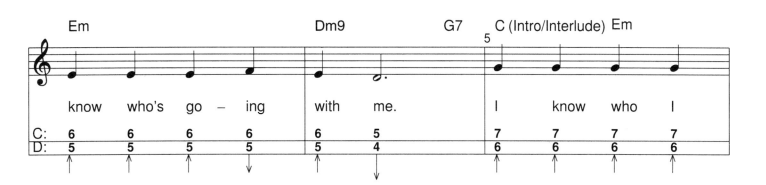

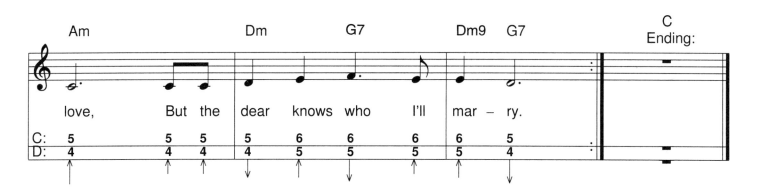

I Never Will Marry

Killarney

Blow ↑; Draw ↓

Michael W. Balfe

Kathleen Mavourneen

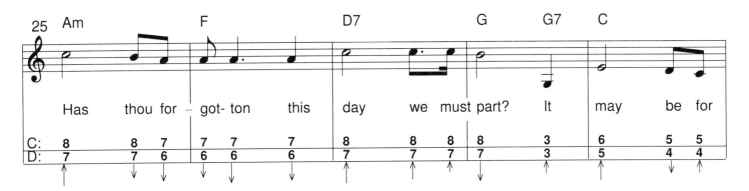

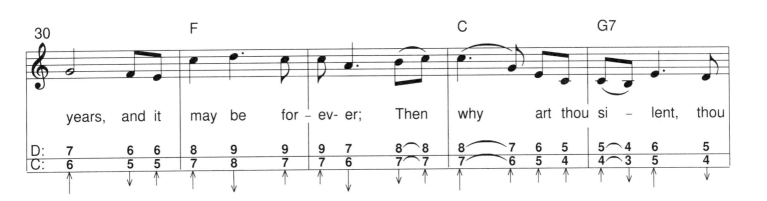

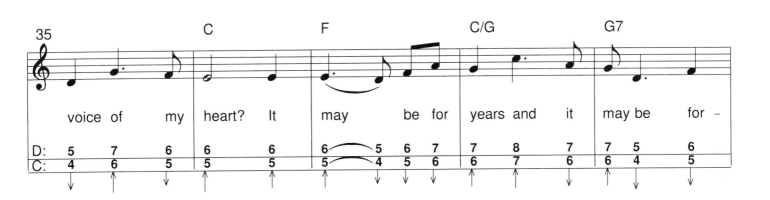

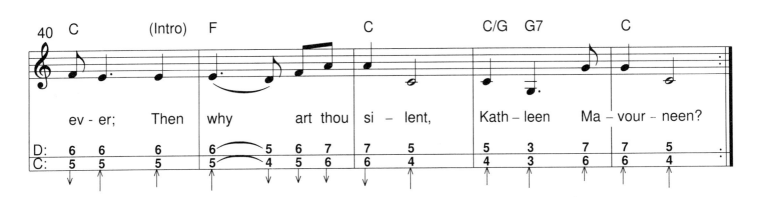

The Last Rose Of Summer
Thomas Moore

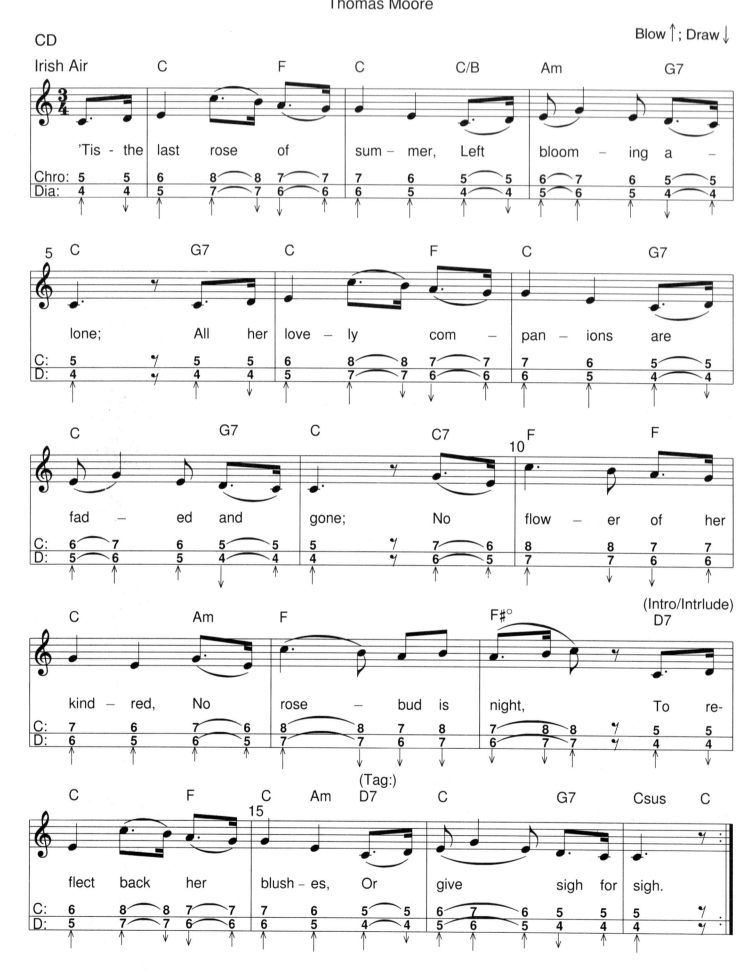

The Minstrel Boy
Thomas Moore

The Londonderry Air

*Melody Maker: G
Country Tuned: C

Blow ↑; Draw ↓

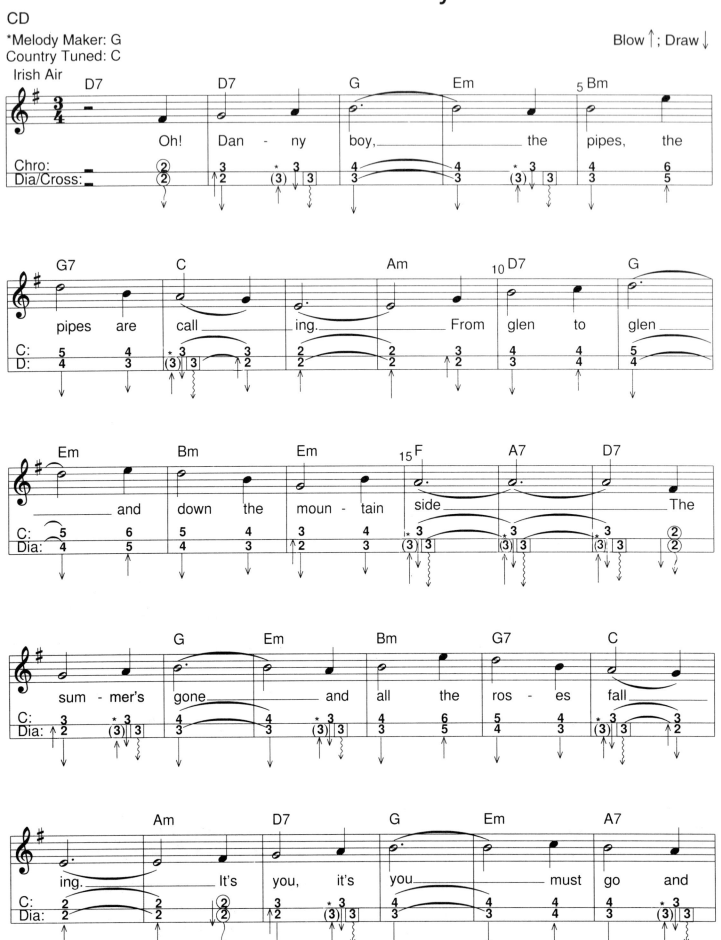

Molly Malone
Cockles and Mussels

Blow ↑ ; Draw ↓

Paddy Works On The Railroad

Blow ↑ ; Draw ↓

The Rose Of Tralee

The Sally Gardens

Shule Aroon
Come, Oh Love

Blow ↑ ; Draw ↓

Ballad

Am F Am C Em F

I wish I were on yon — der hill. 'Tis there I'd sit and

Chro: 2 3 4 4 4 3 3 2 2 3 2 3 3 4 3
Dia: 5 6 7 7 7 6 6 5 5 6 5 6 6 7 6

Em F C Em F

cry my fill, 'Till ev' — ry tear would turn a mill, And

C: 3 2 1 1 2 2 1 1 1 2 2 3 2 4 4
D: 6 5 4 4 5 5 4 4 4 5 5 6 5 7 7

Em Dm Am Am Em F C

safe for aye, my dar — ling be. Come, come, come oh love,
Shule, shule, shule, a - roon.

C: 3 4 3 3 2 1 2 3 3 4 4 3 3 2 2
D: 6 7 6 6 5 4 5 6 6 7 7 6 6 5 5

Em F Em F C

Come quick — ly and soft — ly; Come to the door, and a —

C: 3 2 3 3 4 3 3 2 1 1 2 2 1 1 1 2 2
D: 6 5 6 6 7 6 6 5 4 4 5 5 4 4 4 5 5

Em F C Dm Am

way we'll go, And safe for aye, my dar — ling be.

C: 3 2 4 4 5 6 5 5 3 4 4 3 3 3
D: 6 5 7 7 8 8 8 7 6 7 7 6 6 6

There Is A Gentle Gleam

Blow ↑; Draw ↓

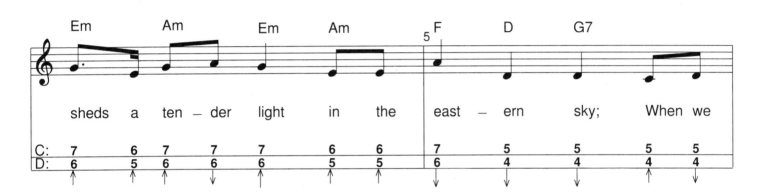

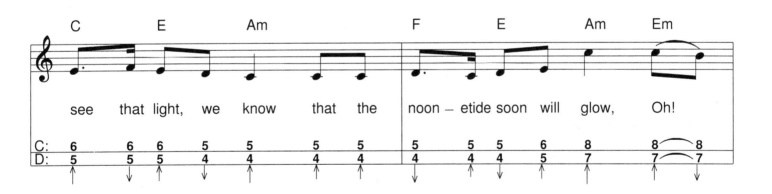

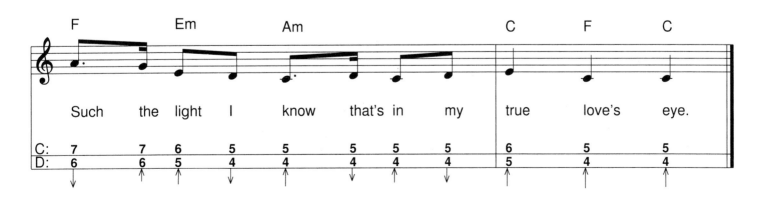

33

Wearing Of The Green

Blow ↑ ; Draw ↓

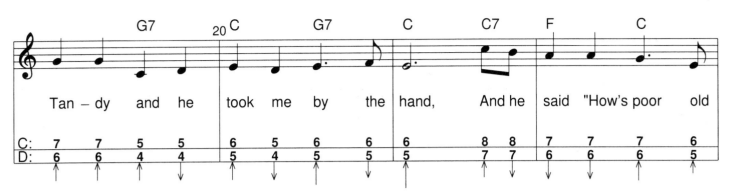

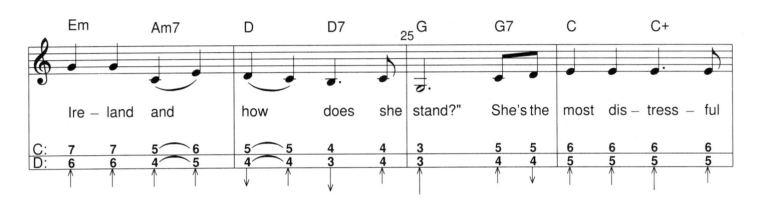

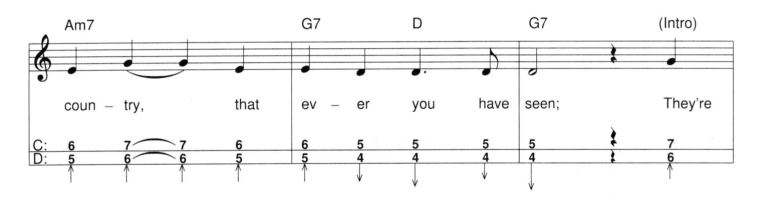

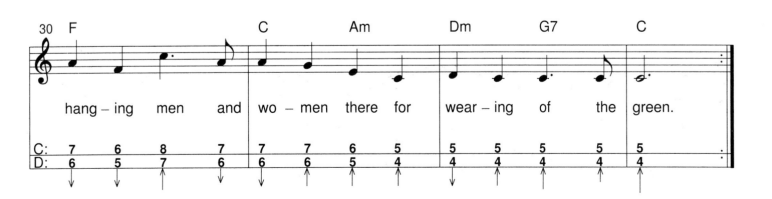

Westering Home

Barney O'Neill

Blow ↑; Draw ↓

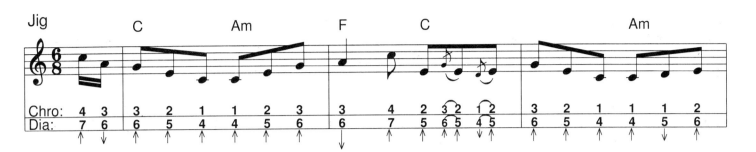

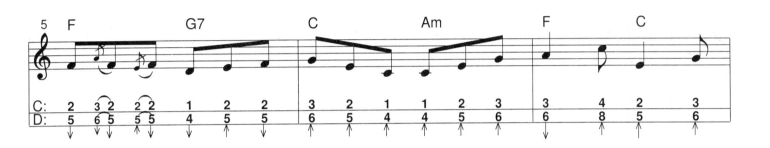

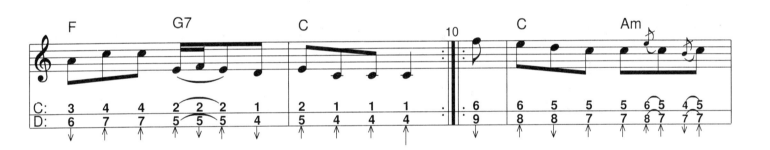

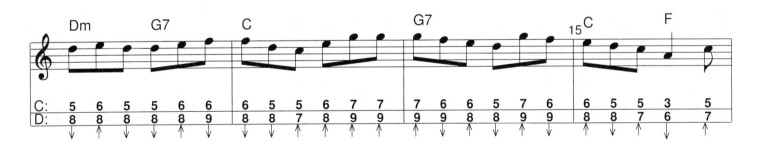

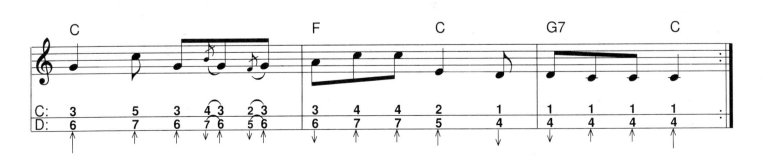

Behind The Bush In The Garden

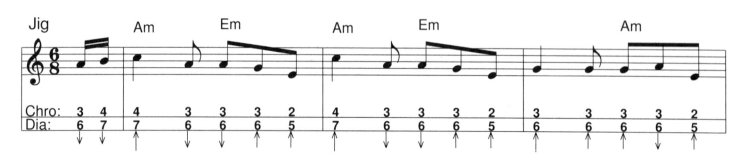

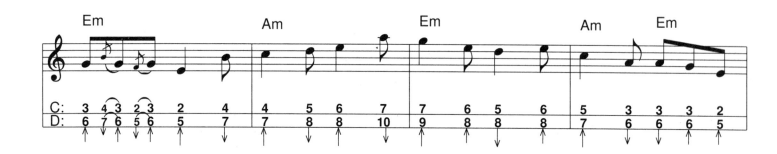

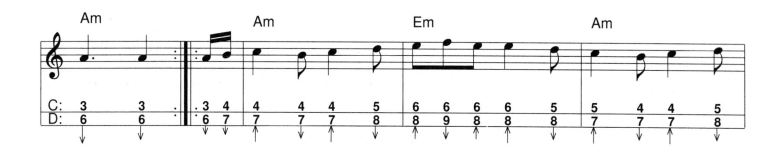

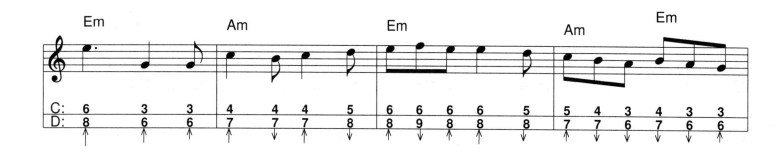

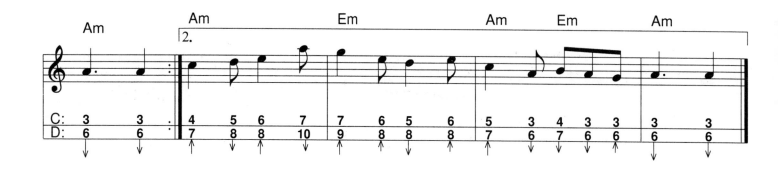

The Black Rogue
(Life is All Checkered)

Blow ↑ ; Draw ↓

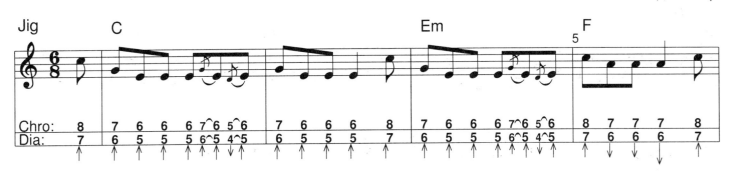

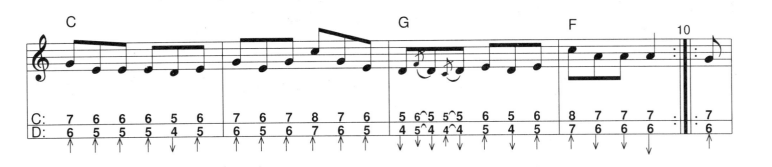

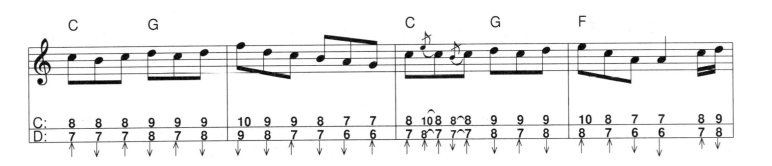

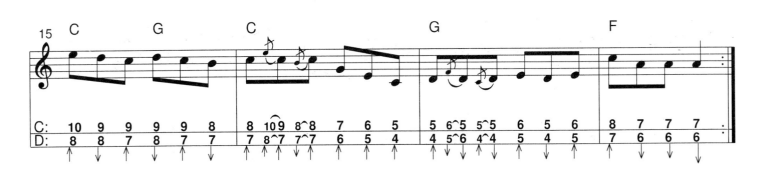

The Blarney Pilgrim

Blow ↑ ; Draw ↓

Blind Billy

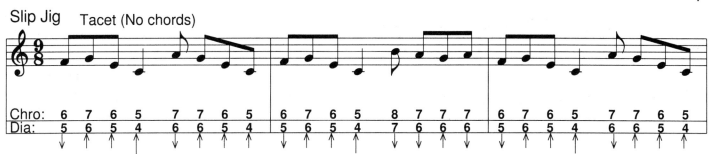

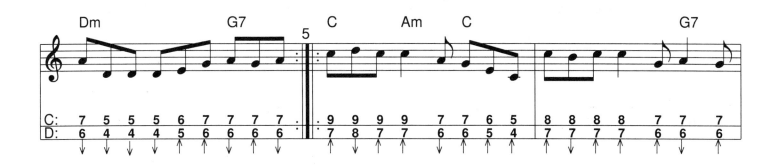

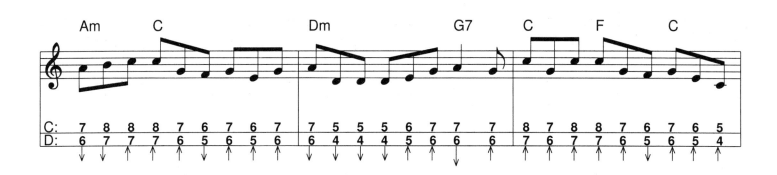

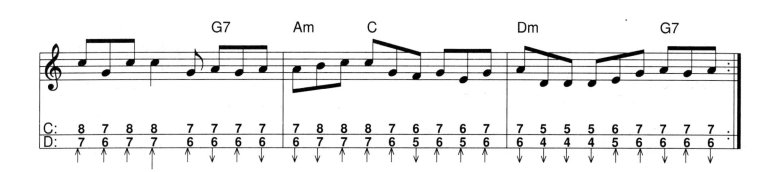

The Cannaughtman's Rambles

The Carraroe

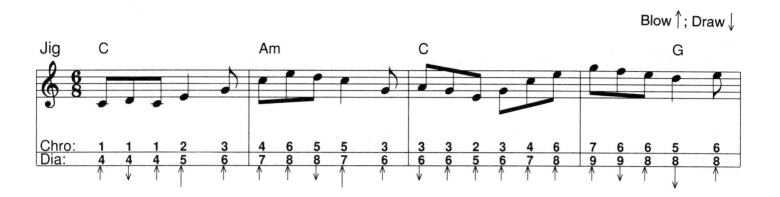

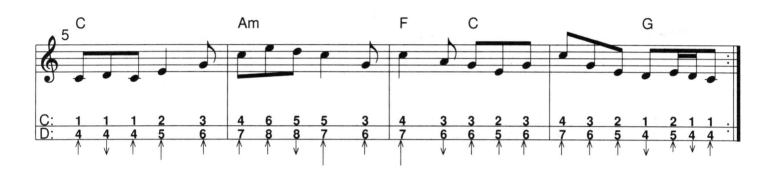

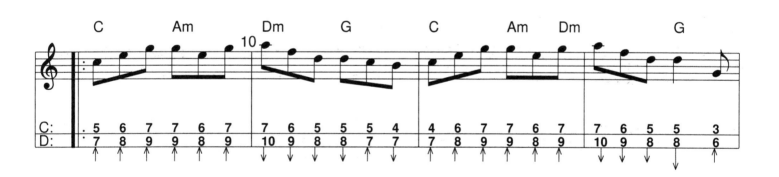

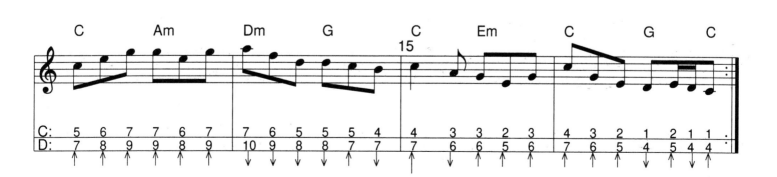

Cherish The Ladies

Blow ↑ ; Draw ↓

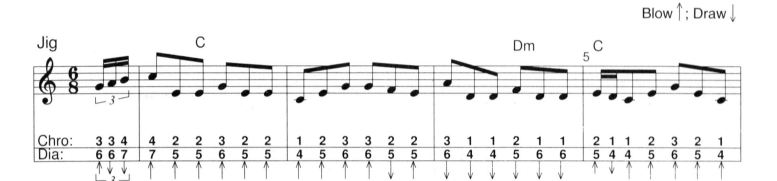

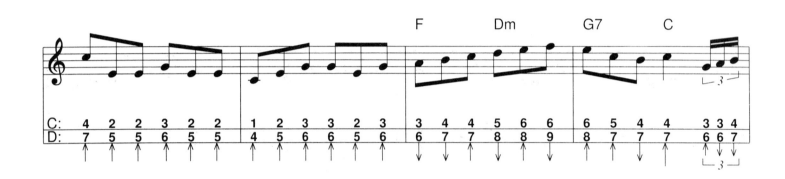

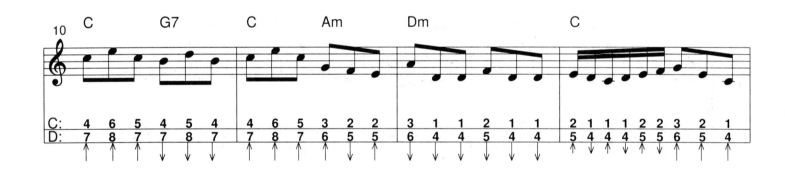

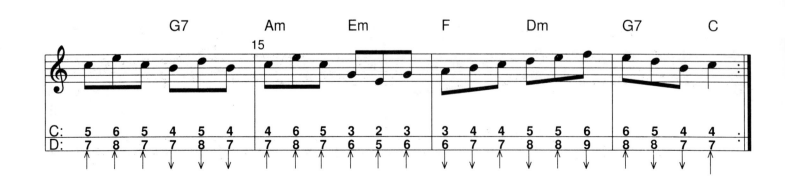

The Dairy Maid

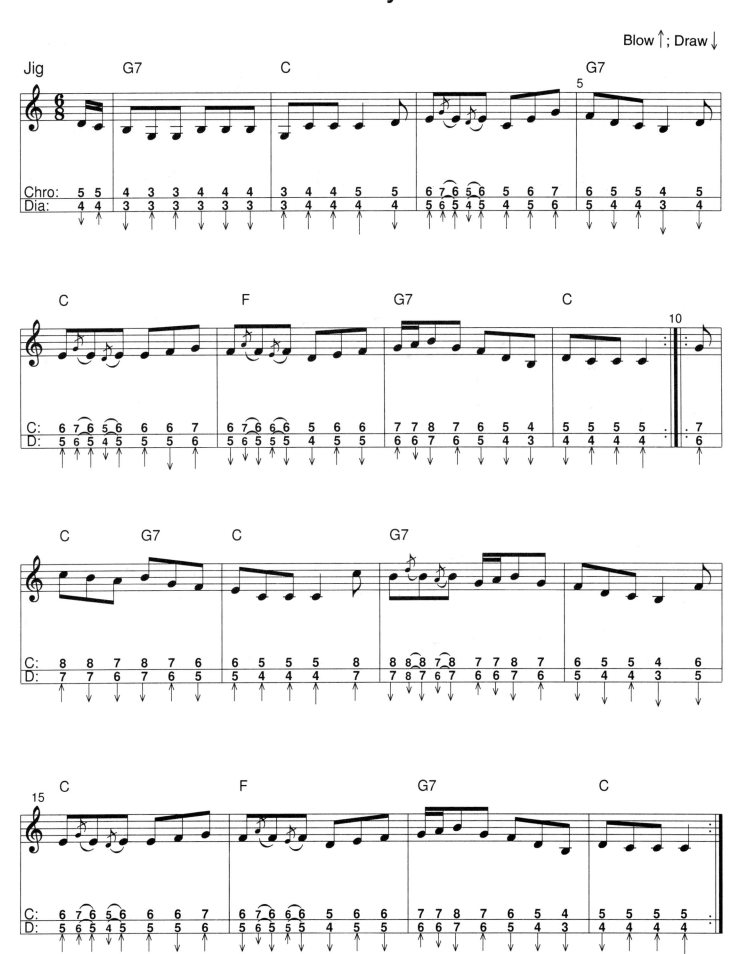

Drops Of Whiskey

Blow ↑ ; Draw ↓

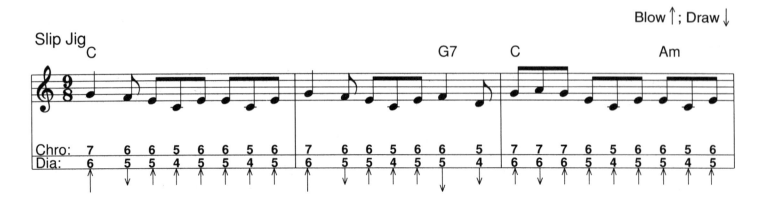

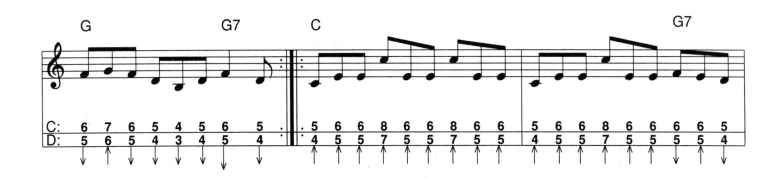

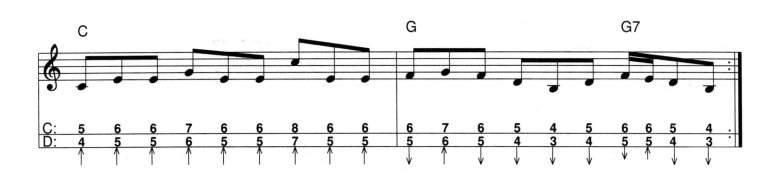

Ellis's Jig

Crosharp: C

Blow ↑; Draw ↓

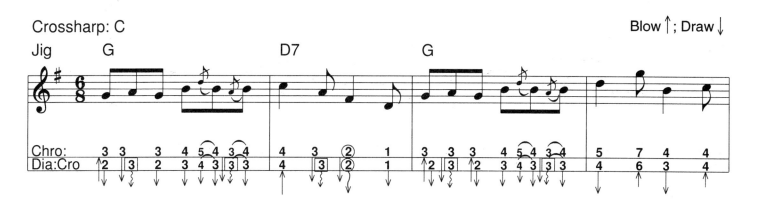

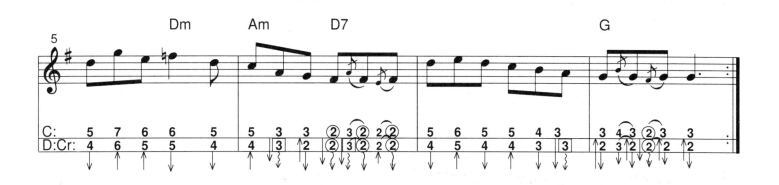

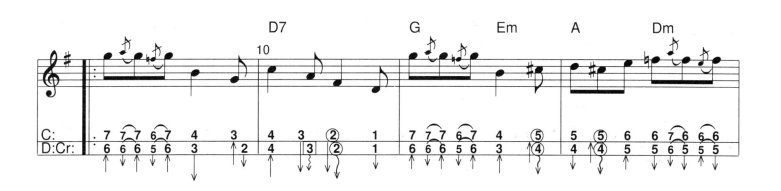

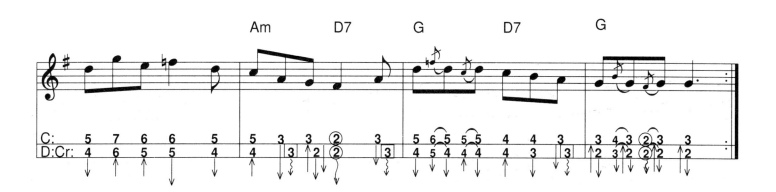

Father Tom's Wager

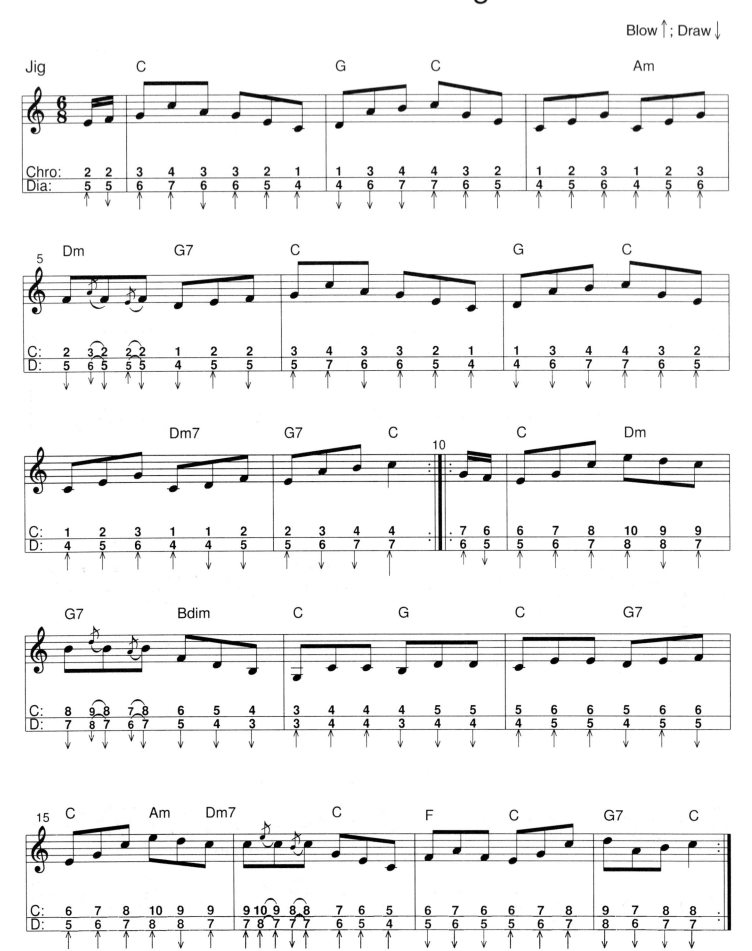

The First Night In America

Blow ↑ ; Draw ↓

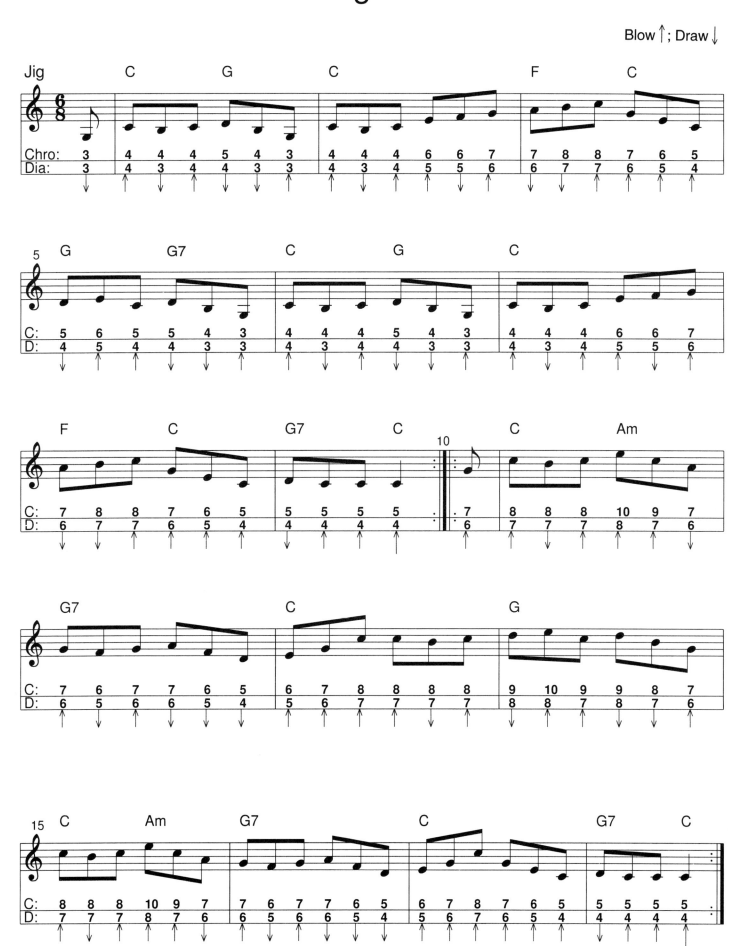

Gary Owen

The Gold Ring

Blow ↑ ; Draw ↓

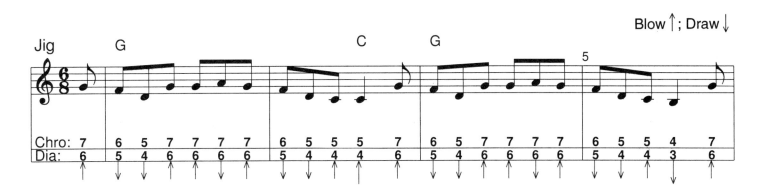

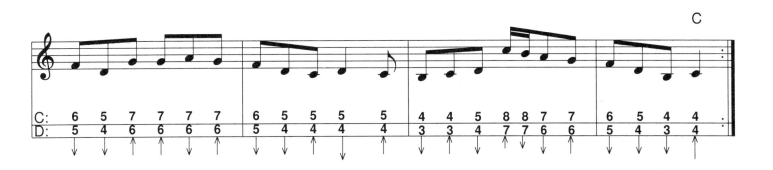

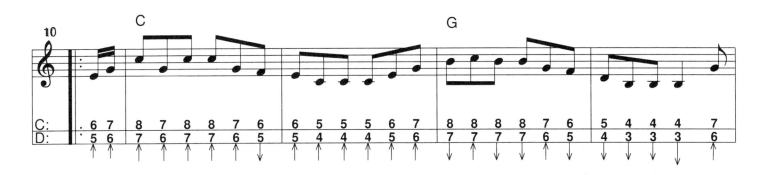

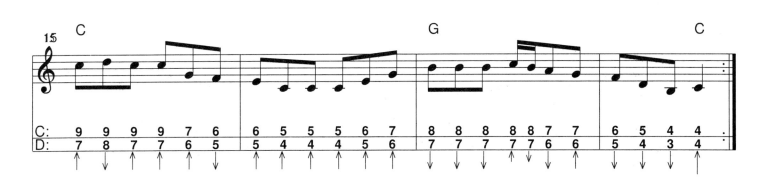

Green Sleeves

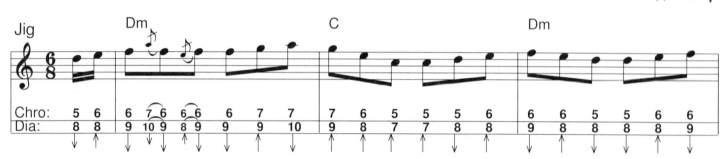

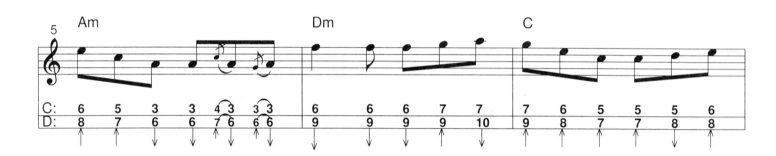

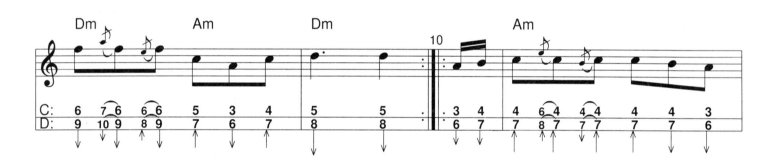

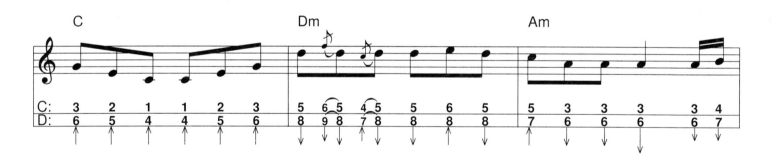

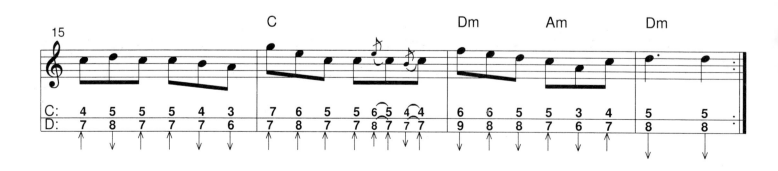

52

The Gudgeon Of Maurice's Car

Haste To The Wedding

Blow ↑ ; Draw ↓

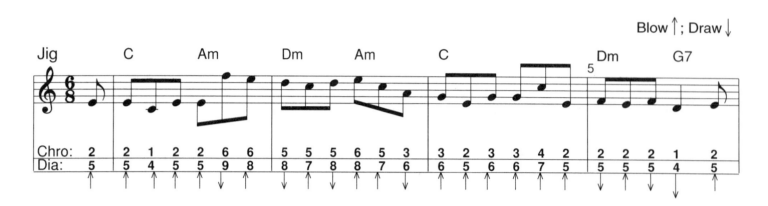

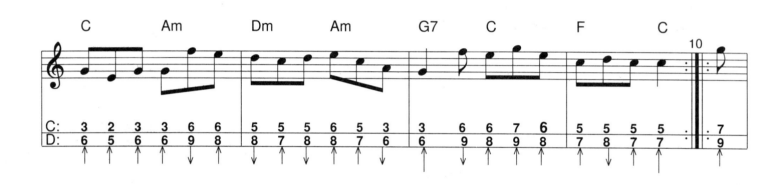

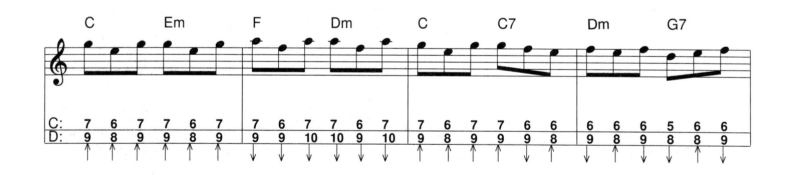

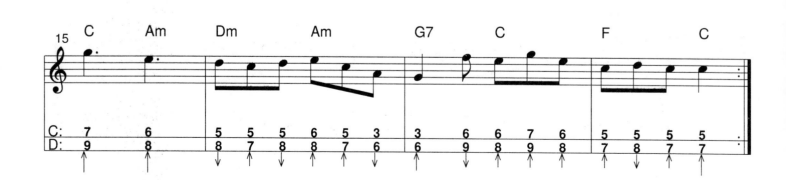

The Highway To Dublin

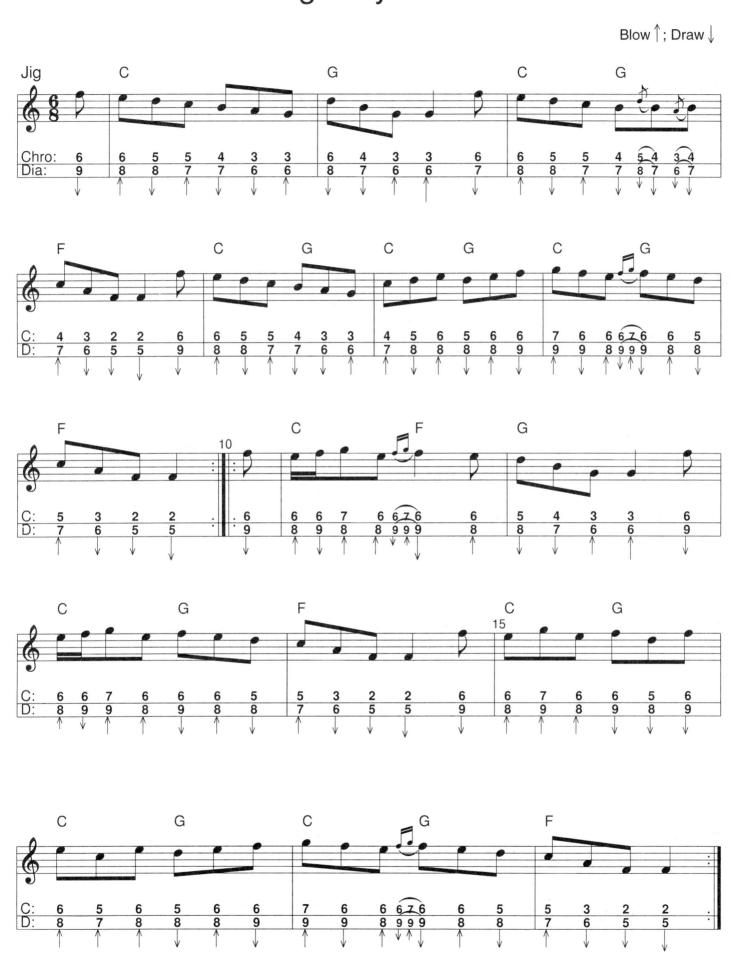

The Humors Of Whiskey

Blow ↑; Draw ↓

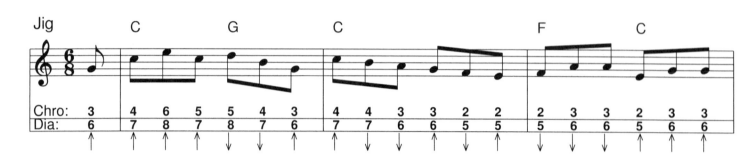

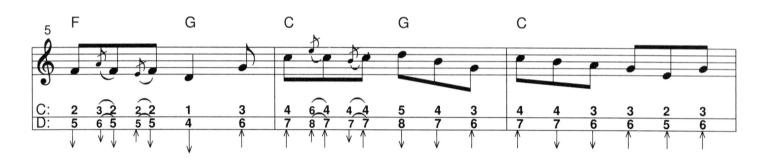

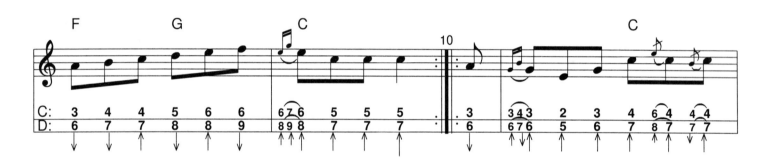

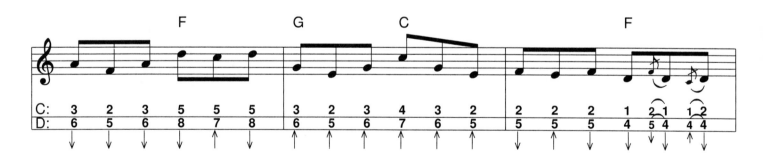

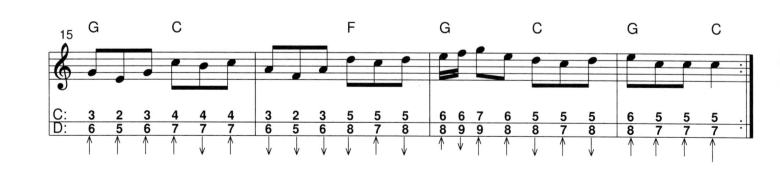

I'll Neither Spin Nor Weave

Blow ↑ ; Draw ↓

The Irish Washerwoman

Blow ↑ ; Draw ↓

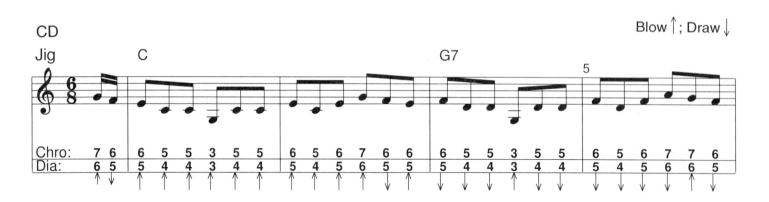

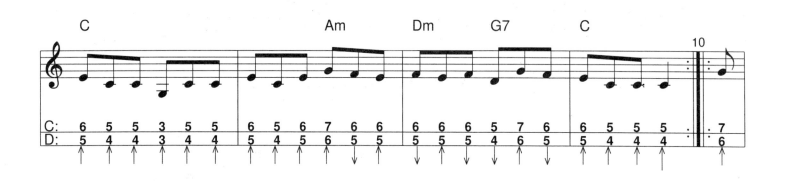

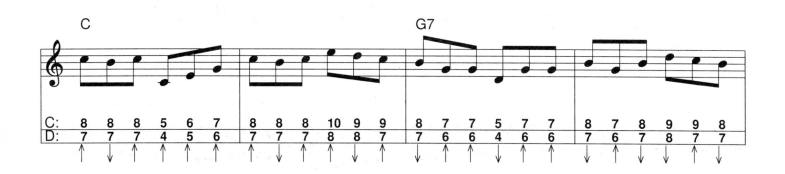

(Intro/Interlude)

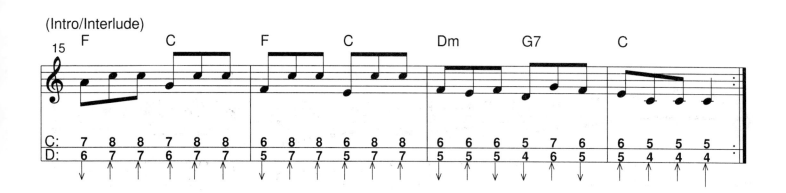

Jennie's Chickens

Blow ↑ ; Draw ↓

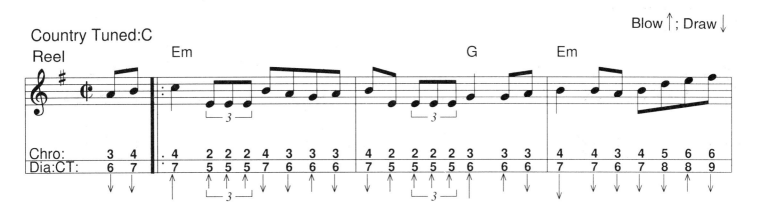

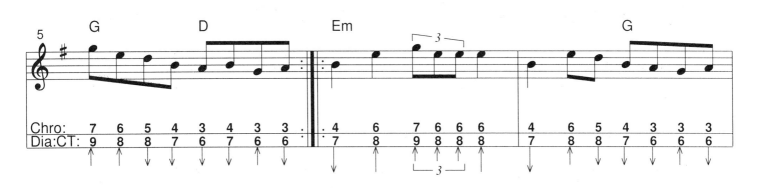

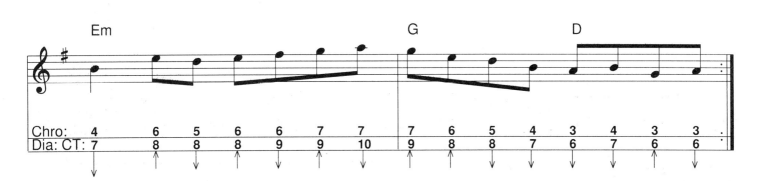

Katie's Fancy

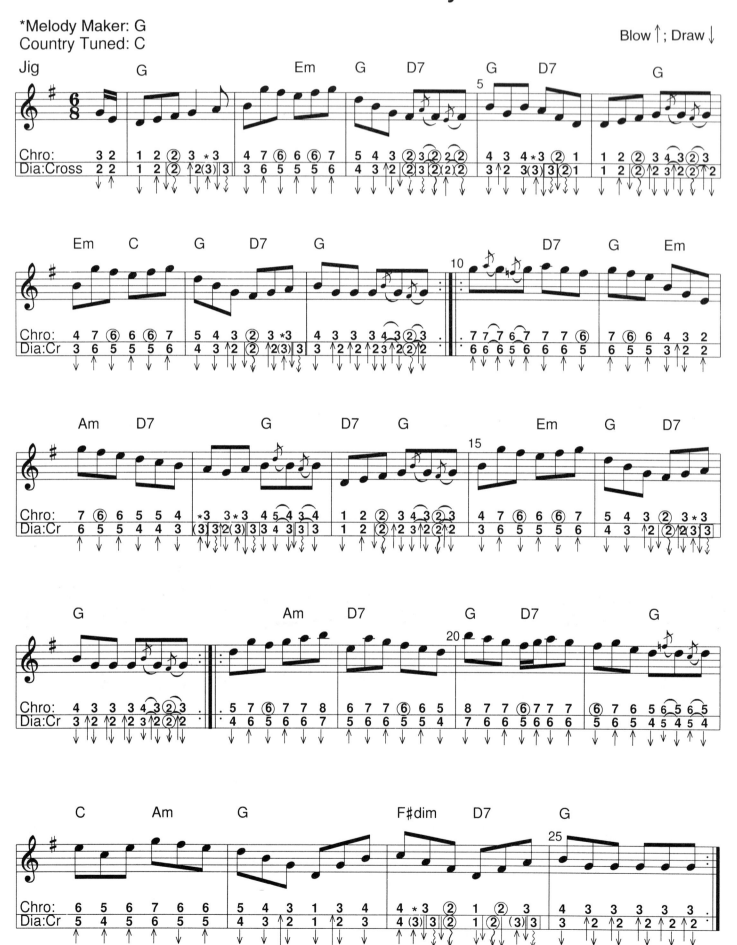

Light And Airy

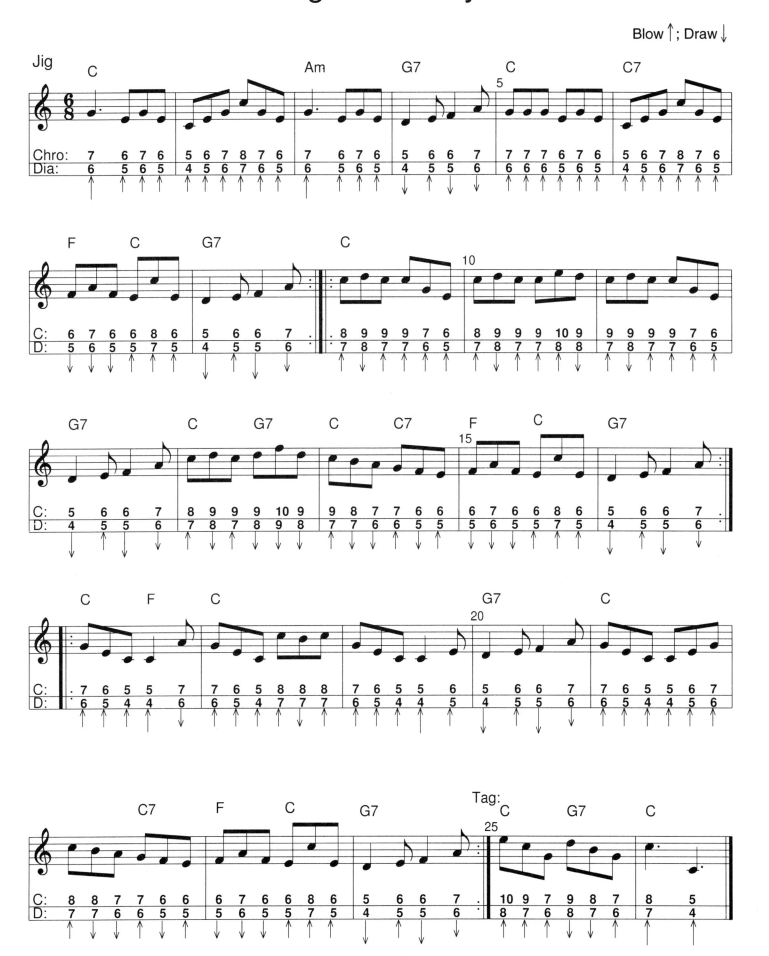

Malowney's Wife

My Darling Asleep

63

O'Gallagher's Frolics

*Melody Maker: G
Country Tuned: C

Blow ↑; Draw ↓

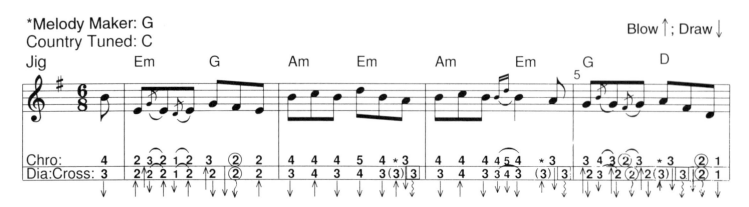

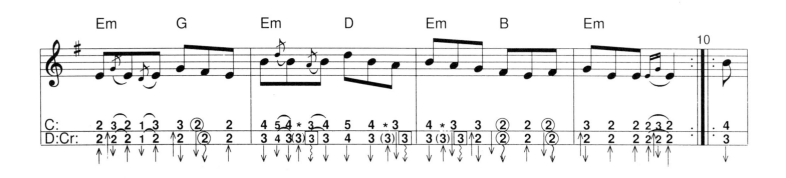

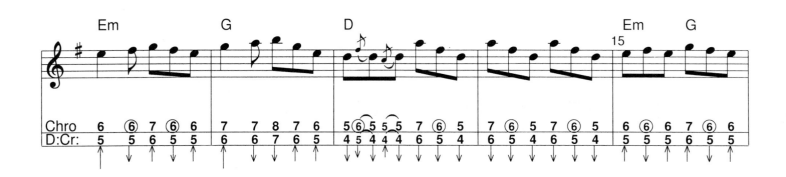

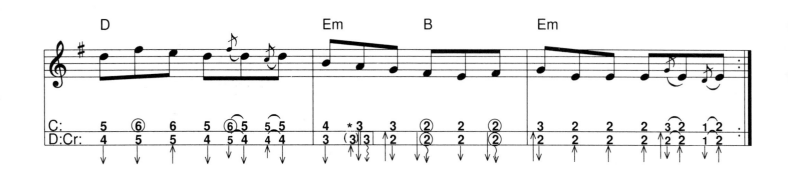

Paddy Whack

Padraic O'Keeffe's

66

Pet Of the Pipers

Blow ↑ ; Draw ↓

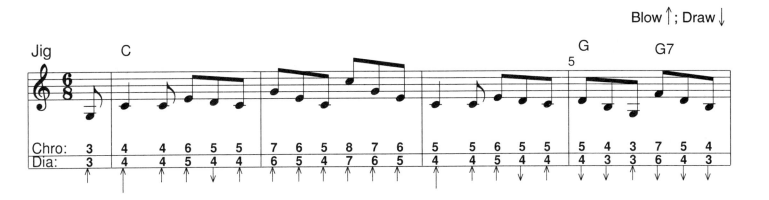

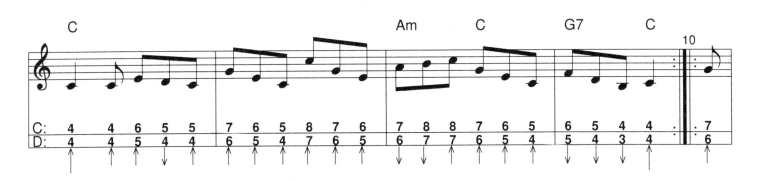

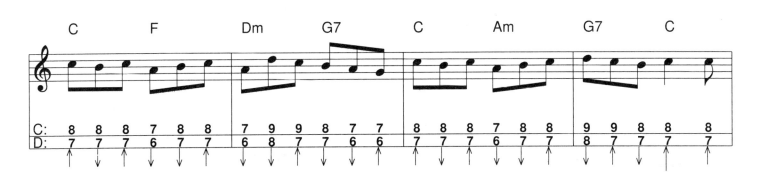

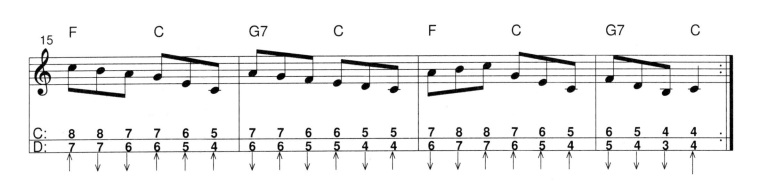

The Priest And His Boots

Blow ↑ ; Draw ↓

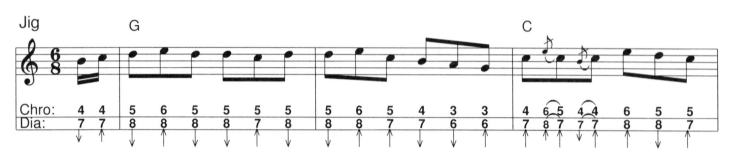

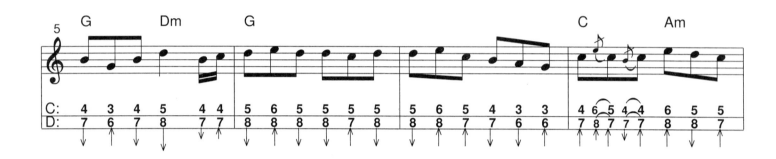

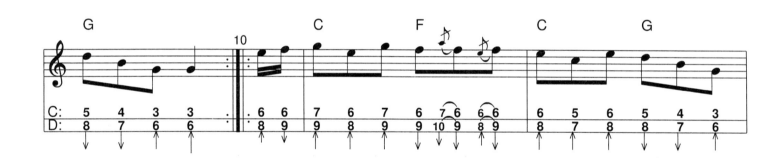

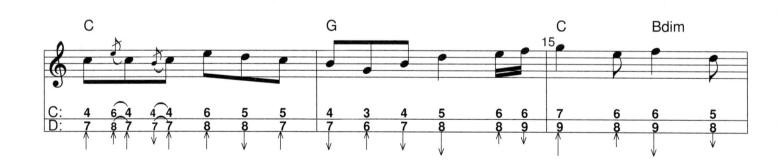

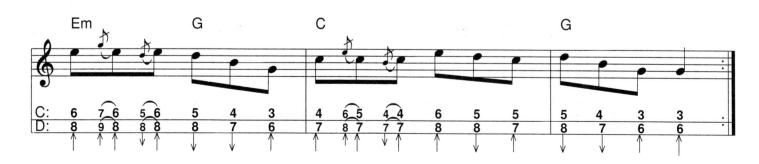

Rathawaun

Blow ↑; Draw ↓

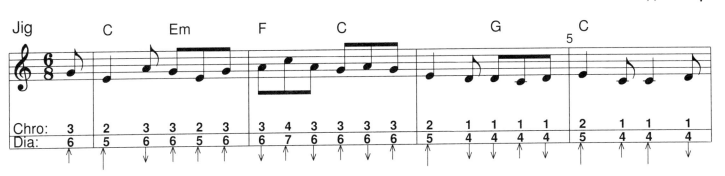

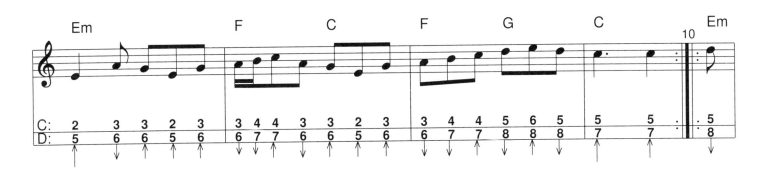

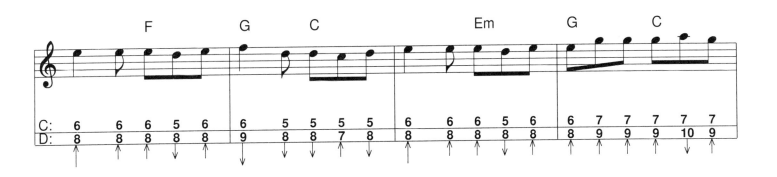

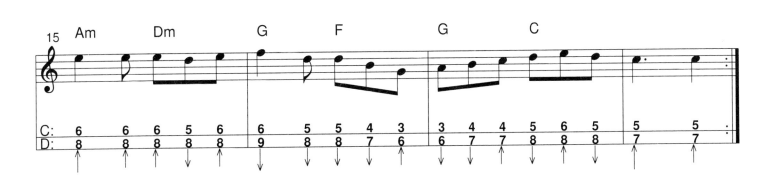

69

The Rocky Road To Dublin

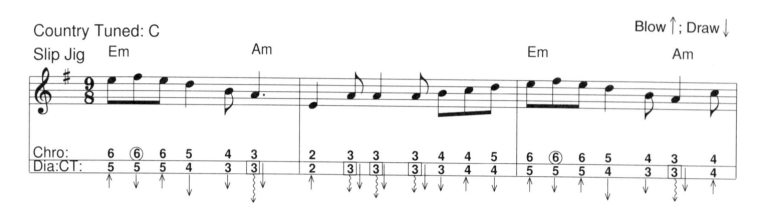

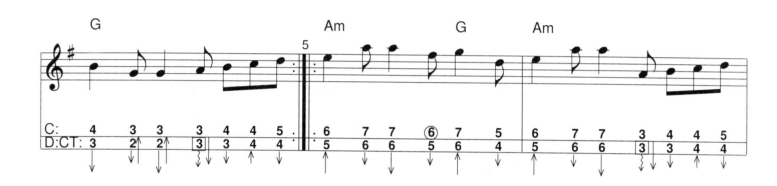

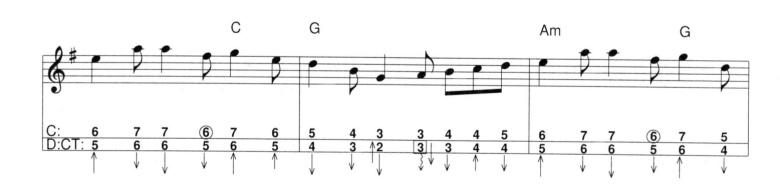

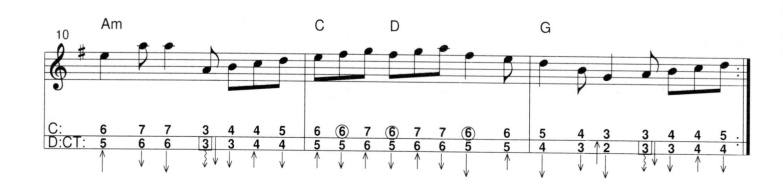

Saddle The Pony

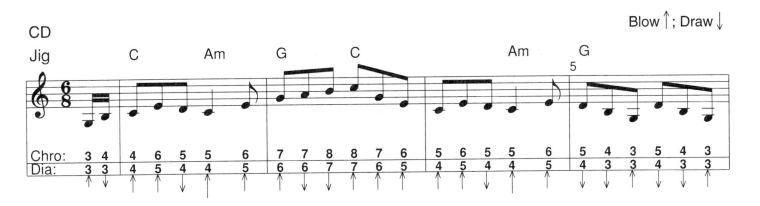

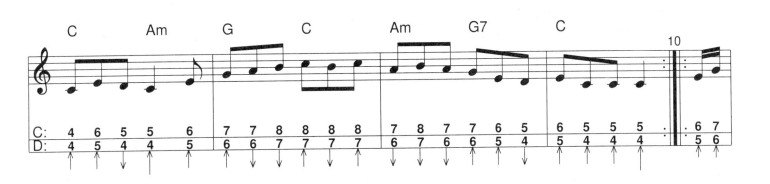

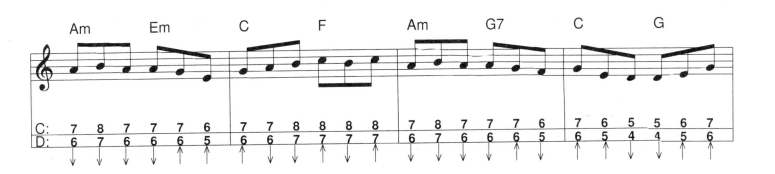

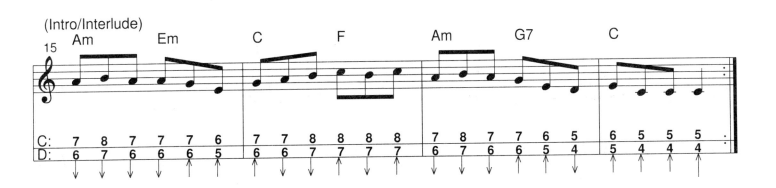

Smash The Windows

The Swallowtail Jig

Blow ↑ ; Draw ↓

Sweet Biddy Daly

The Ten Penny Bit

Blow ↑; Draw ↓

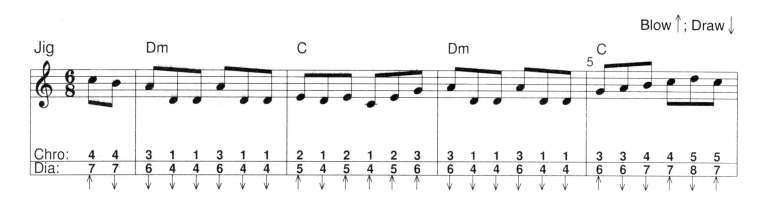

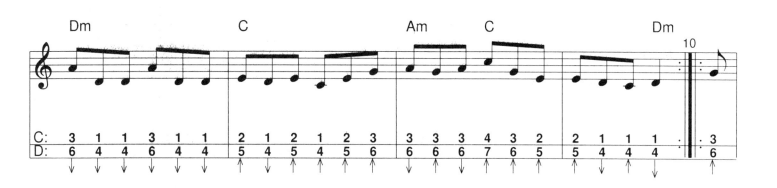

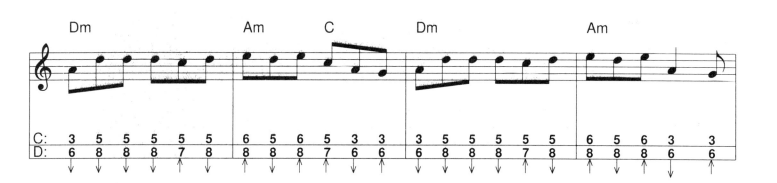

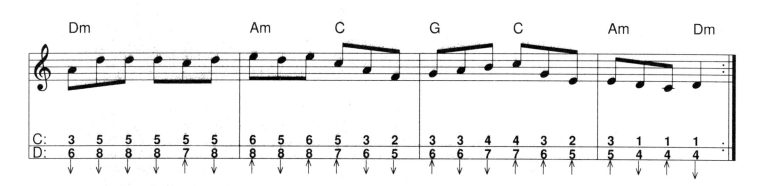

Ten Penny Money

Blow ↑ ; Draw ↓

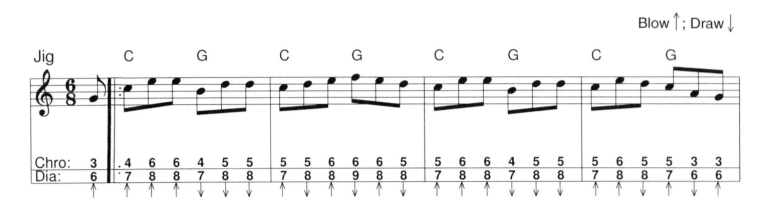

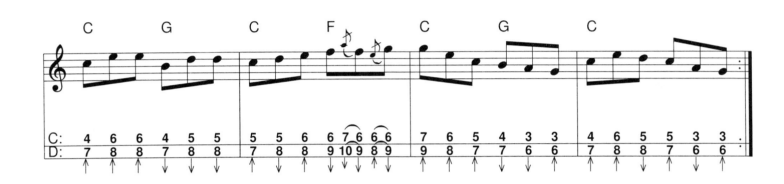

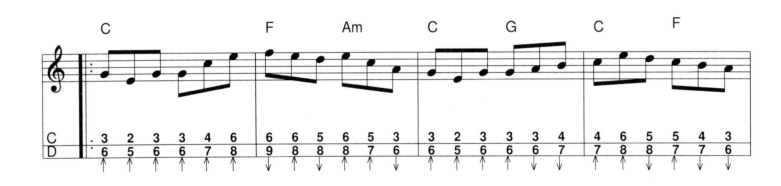

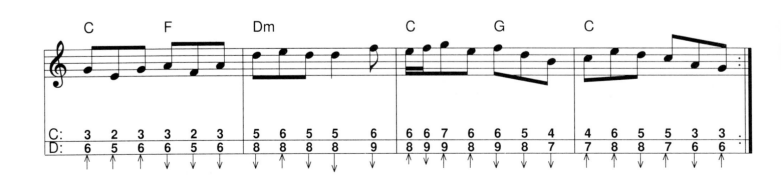

Tobin's Favorite

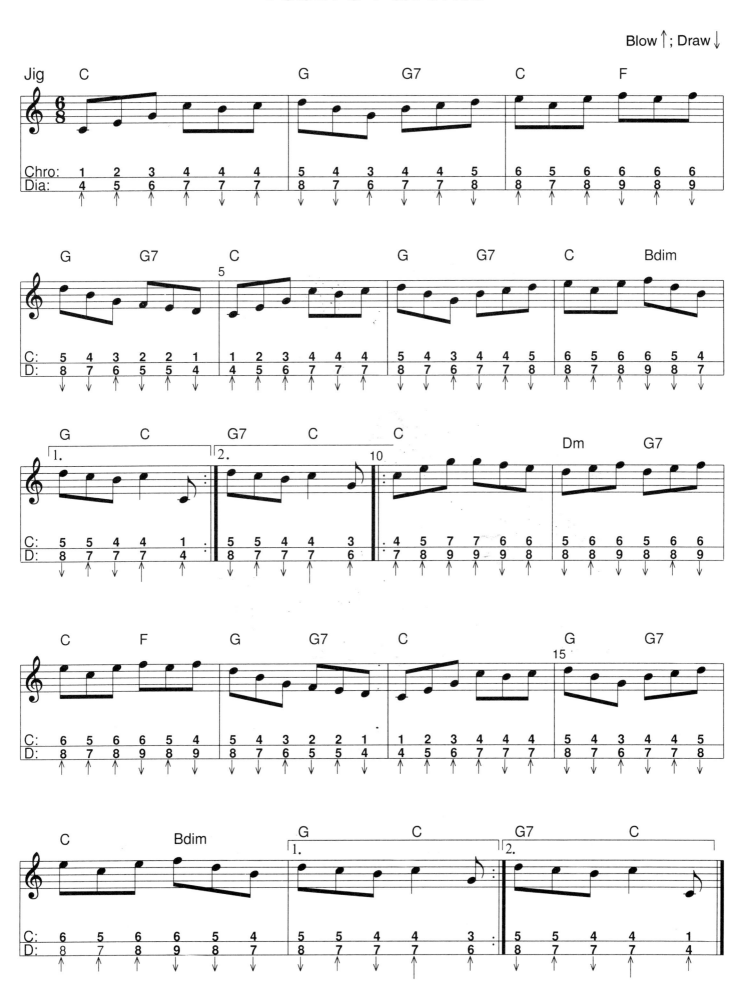

77

Ballinasloe Fair

Blow ↑; Draw ↓

The Blackberry Blossom

79

The Blackthorn Stick

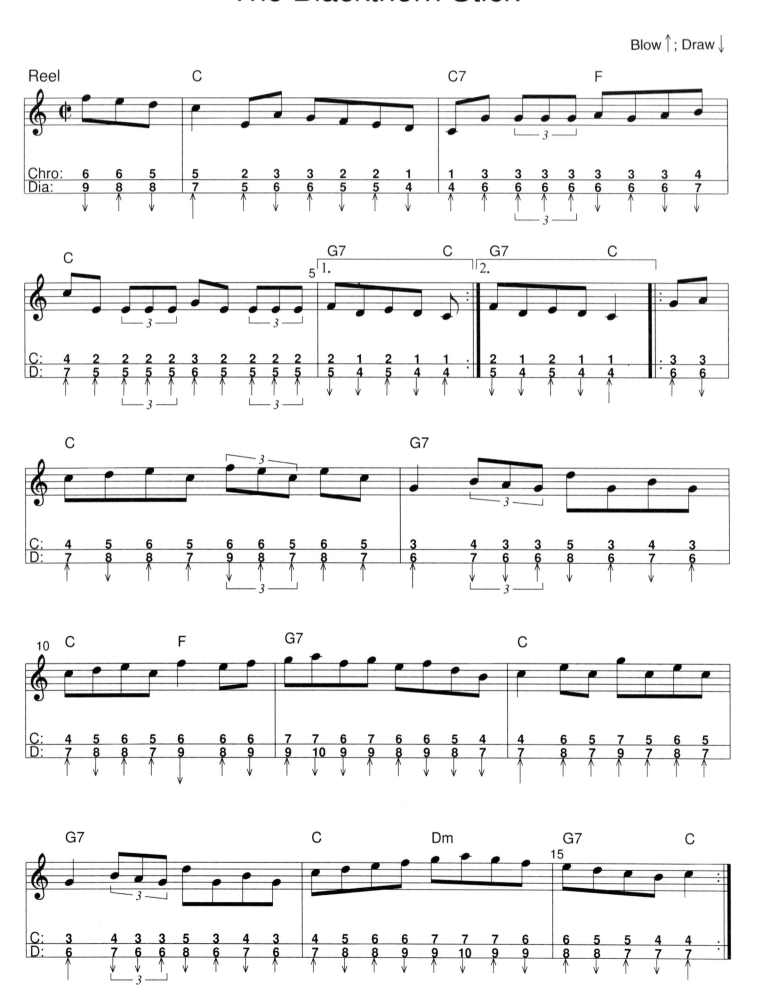

Captain O'Neill

Blow ↑; Draw ↓

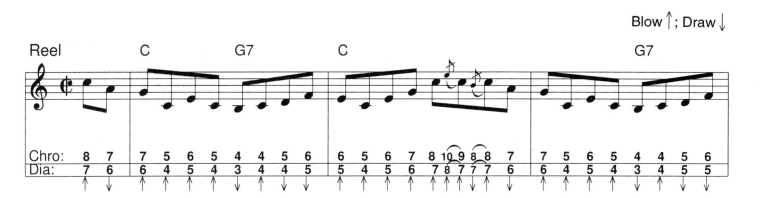

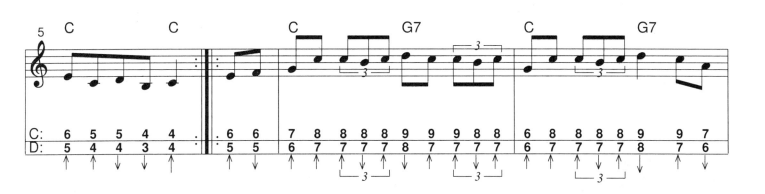

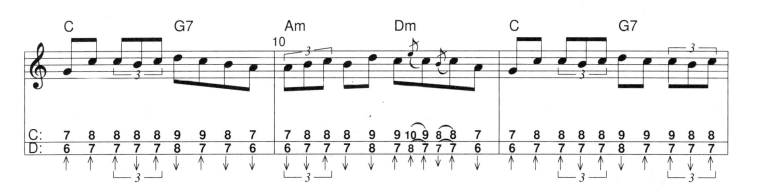

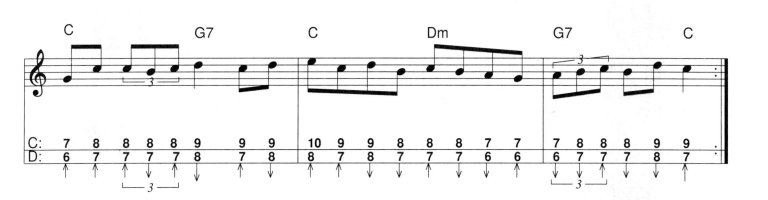

Crowley's Reels

Dan McCarthy's Fancy

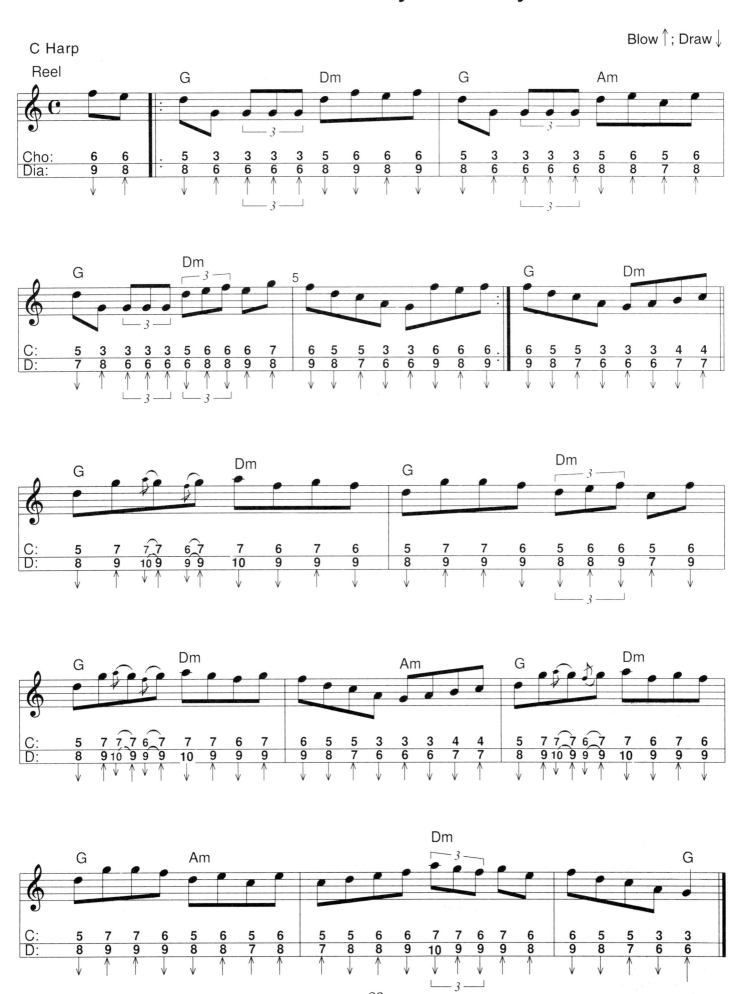

The Flax In Bloom

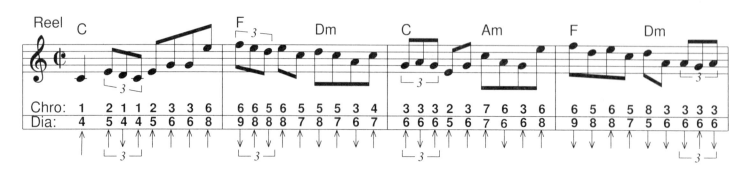

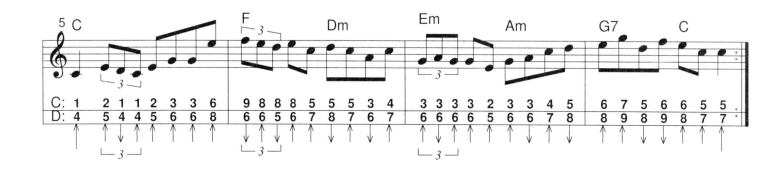

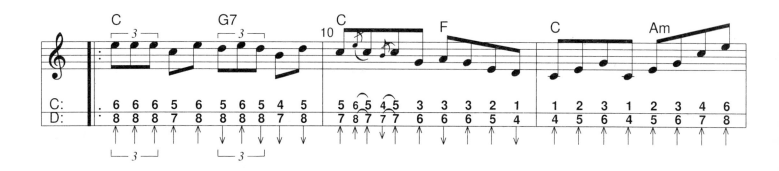

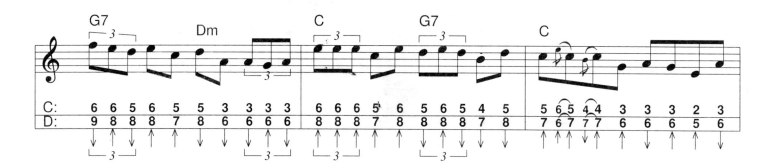

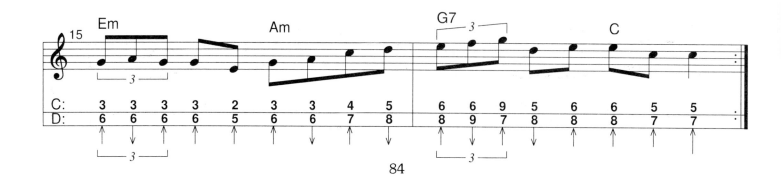

The Flowing Bowl

Blow ↑ ; Draw ↓

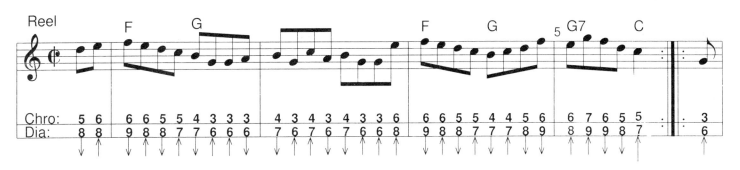

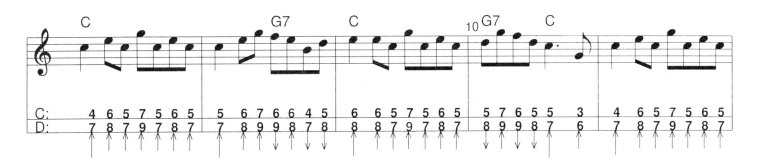

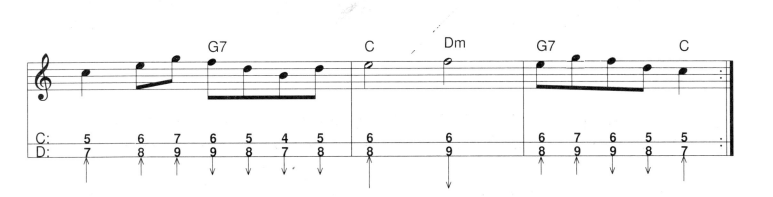

George White's Favorite

The Girl I Left Behind Me

CD

Country Tuned: C

Blow ↑; Draw ↓

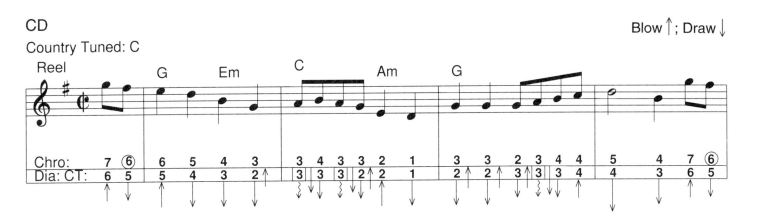

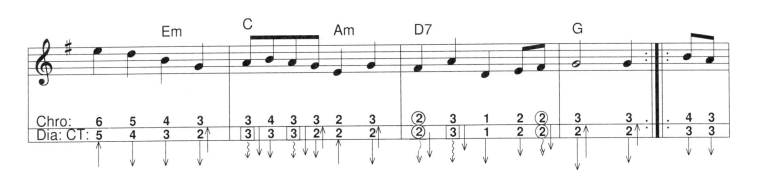

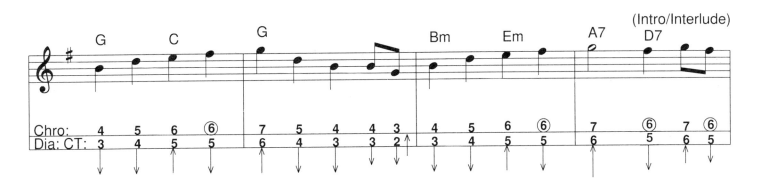

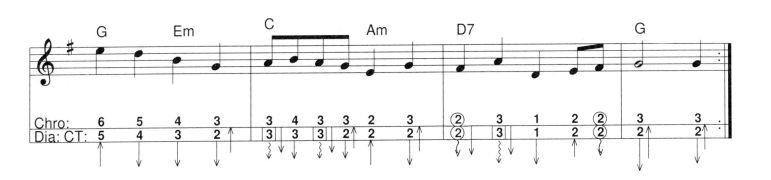

The Green Groves Of Erin

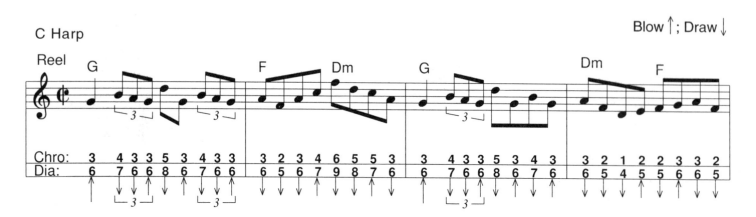

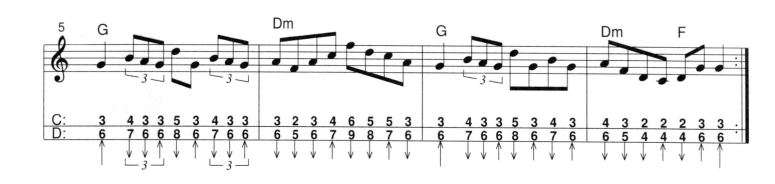

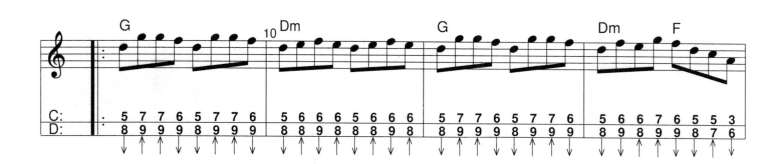

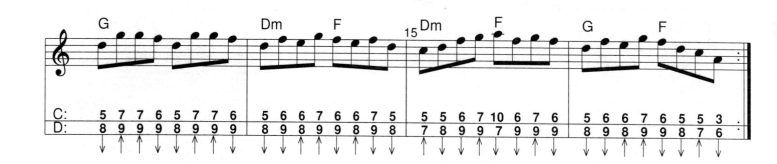

The Green Meadow

Blow ↑ ; Draw ↓

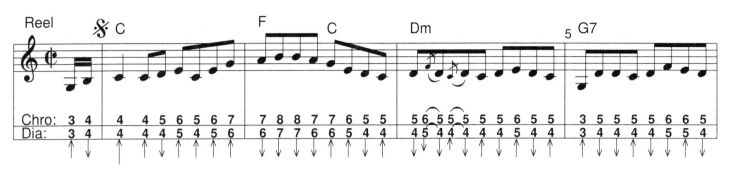

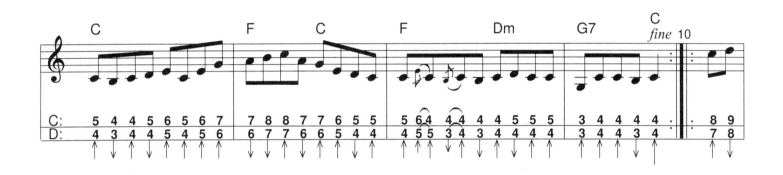

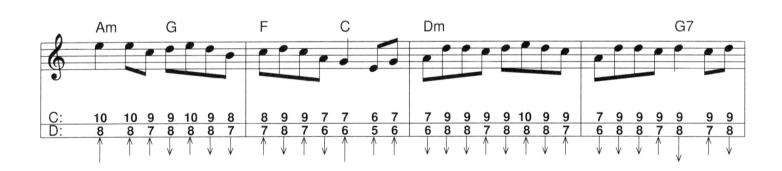

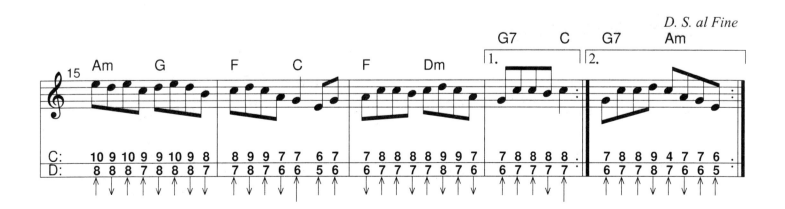

The Grey Daylight

Blow ↑ ; Draw ↓

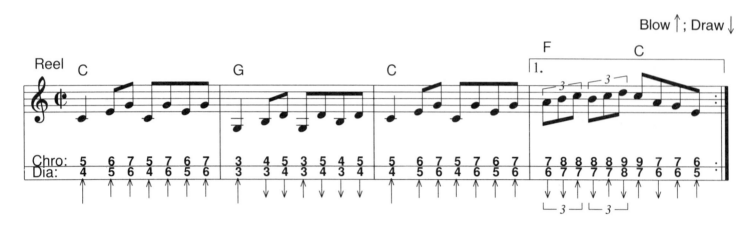

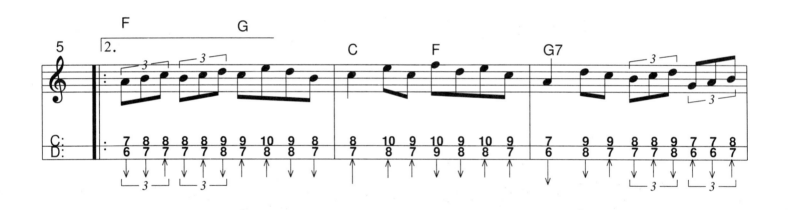

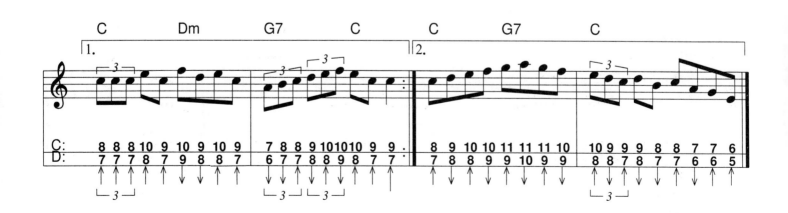

The Hornless Cow

Blow ↑; Draw ↓

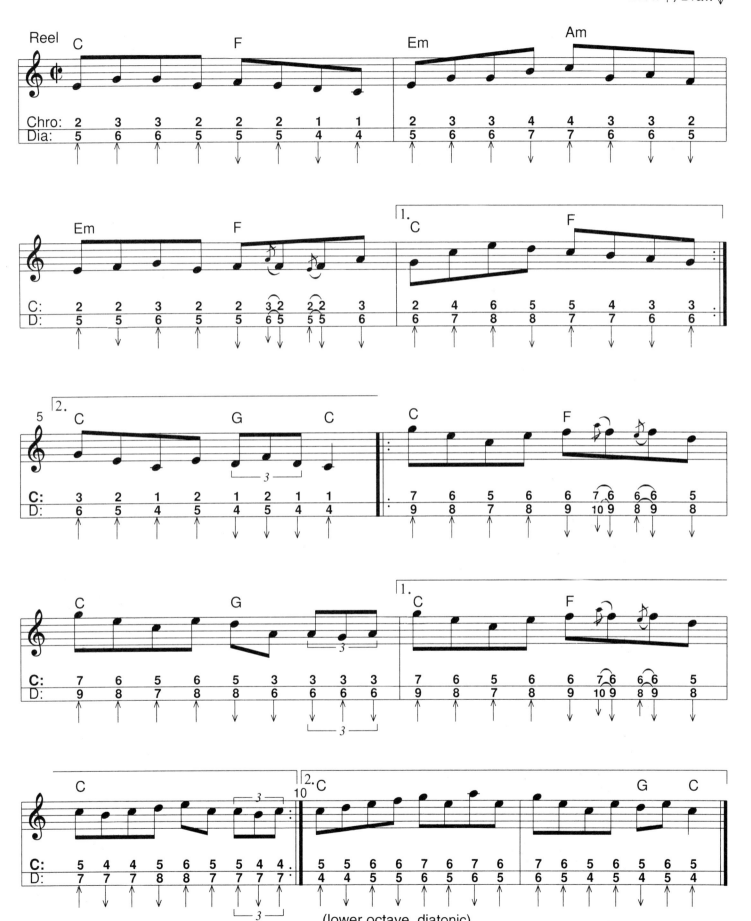

(lower octave, diatonic)

Jenny Picking Cockles

Melody Maker : G

Blow ↑ ; Draw ↓

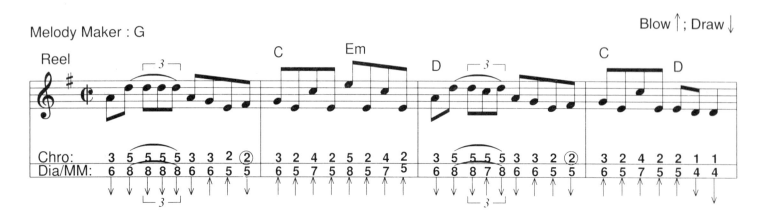

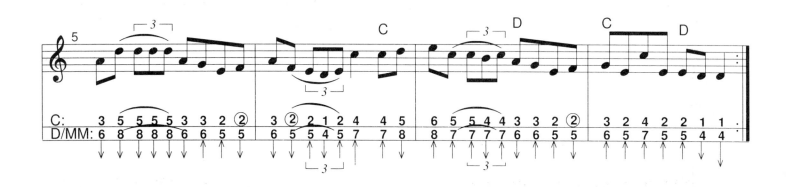

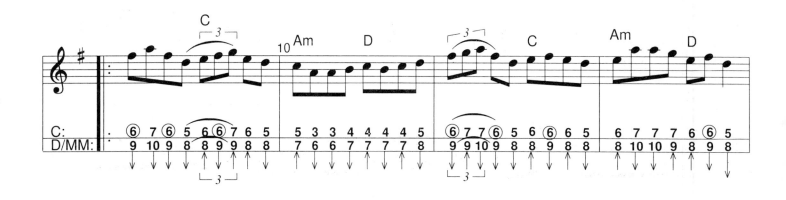

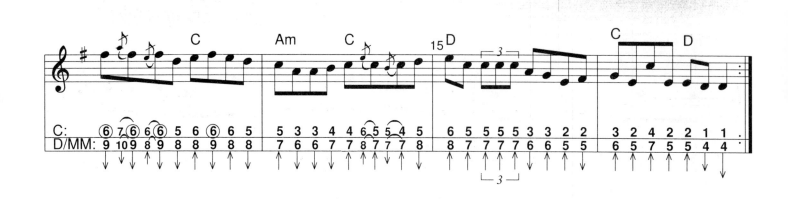

Mason's Apron

The Merry Blacksmith

Blow ↑ ; Draw ↓

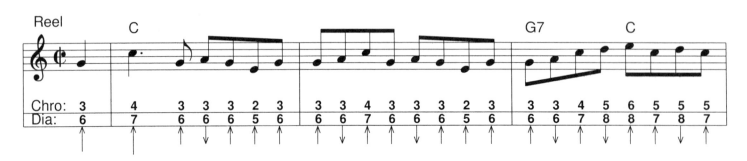

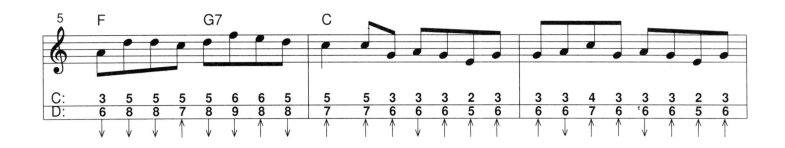

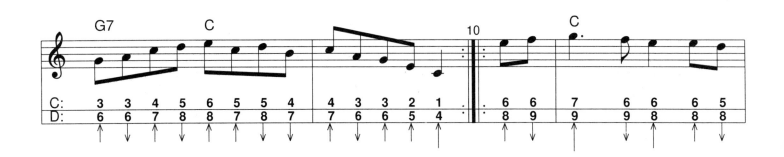

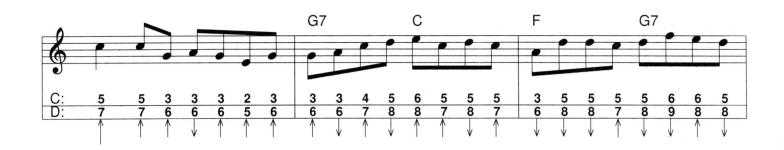

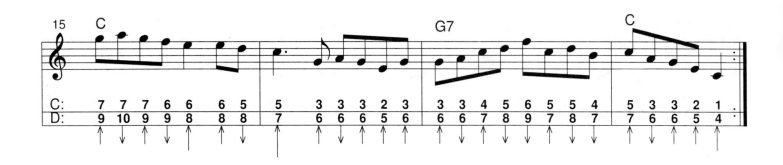

The Merry Harriers

Blow ↑ ; Draw ↓

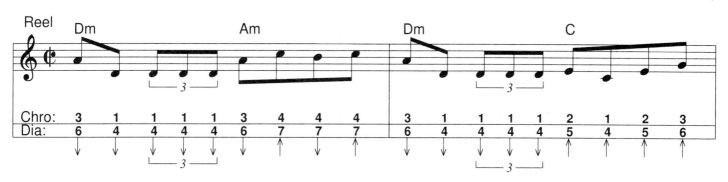

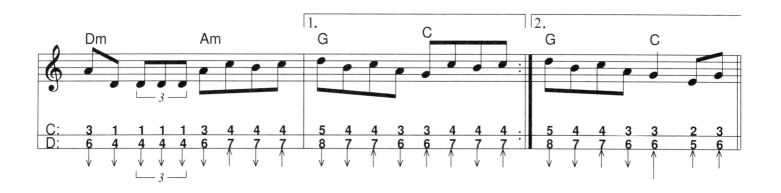

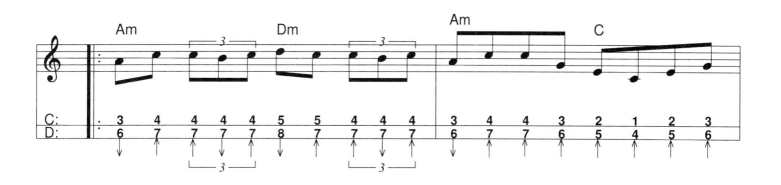

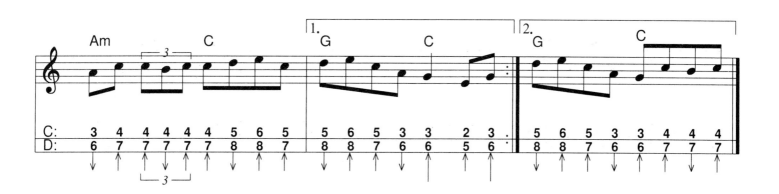

Miss McLeod's Reel

Blow ↑ ; Draw ↓

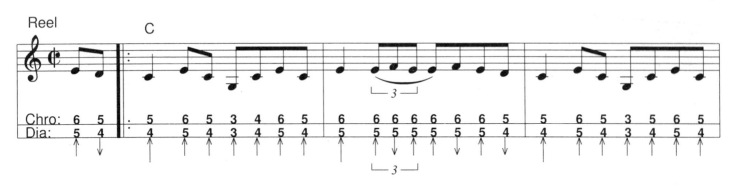

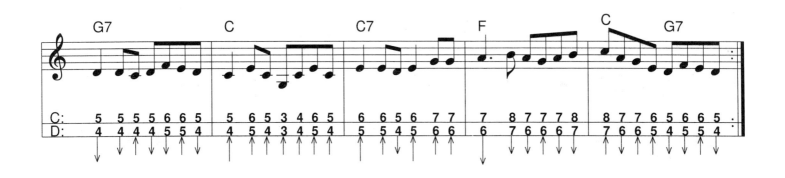

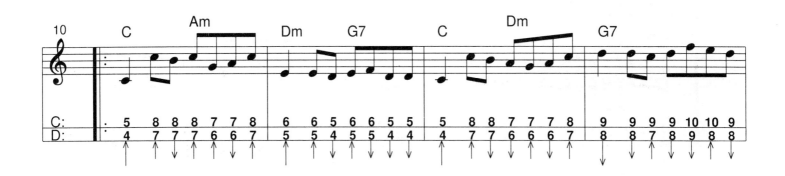

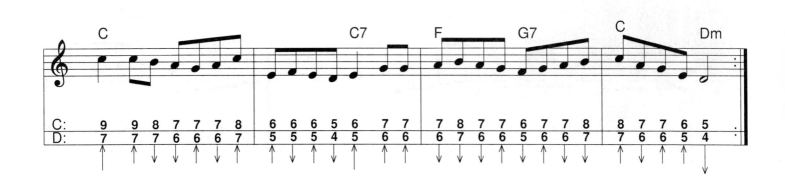

96

Mollie McCarthy

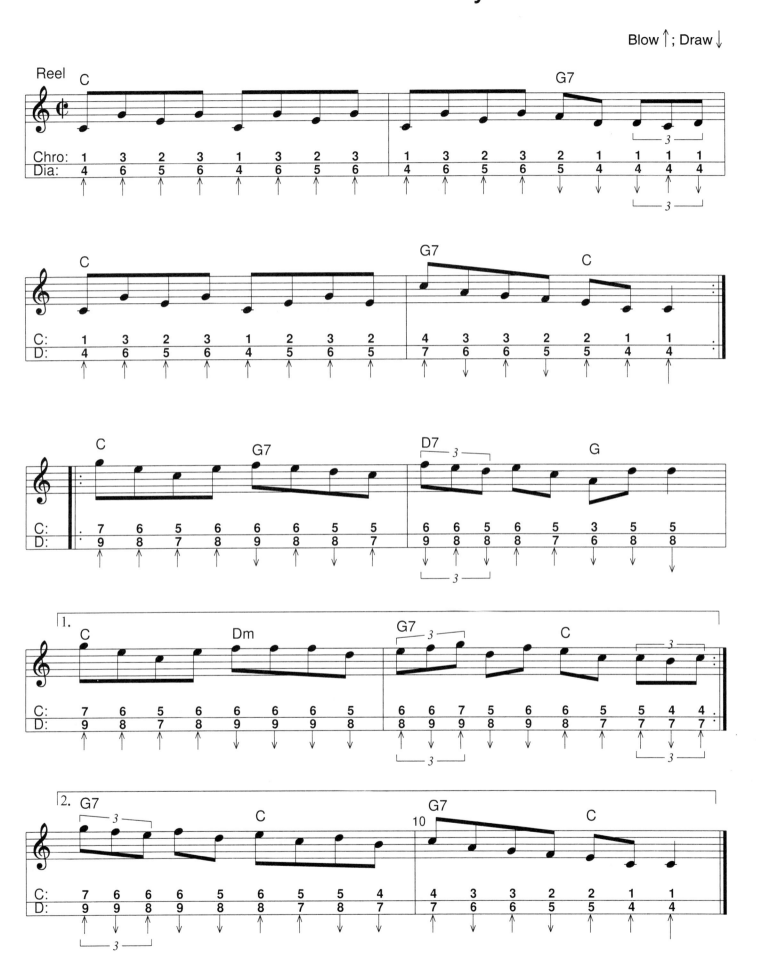

The Mountain Road

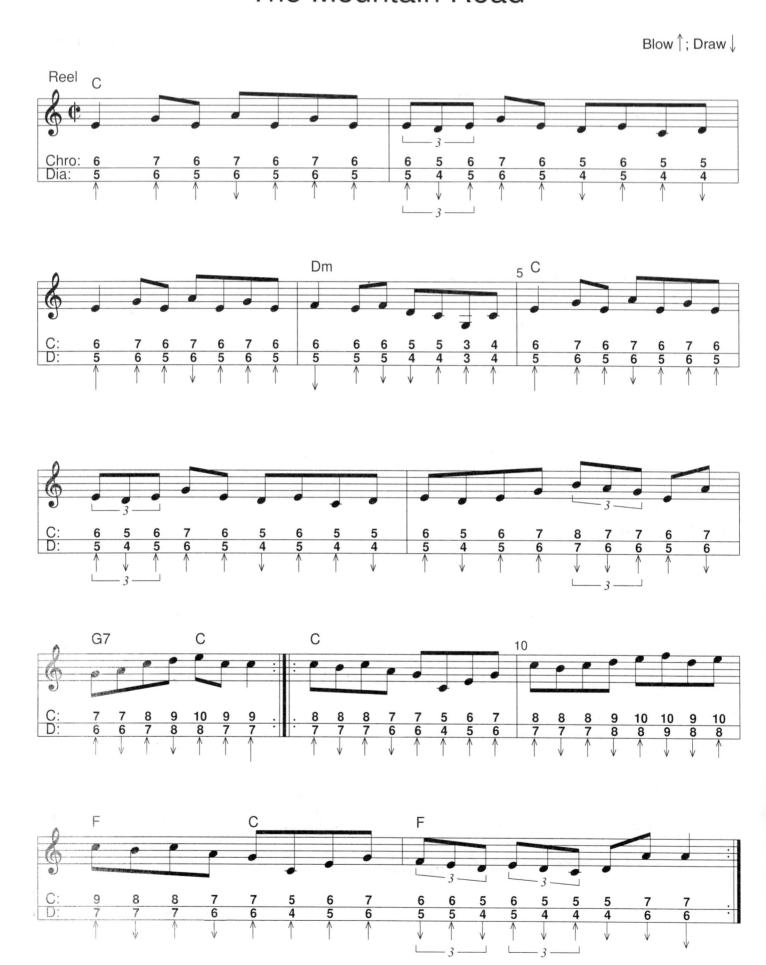

98

The Pigeon On The Gate

Ships Are Sailing

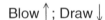

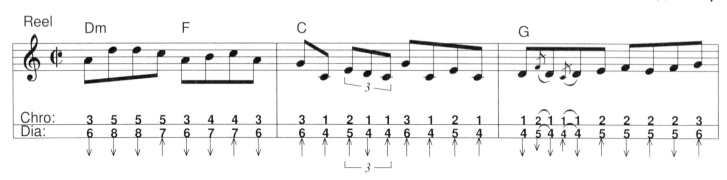

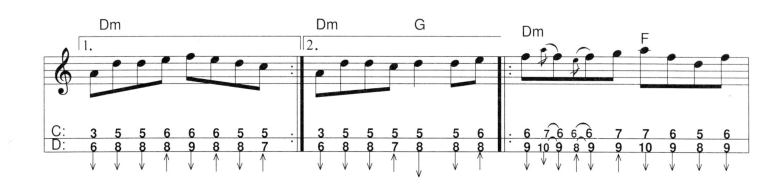

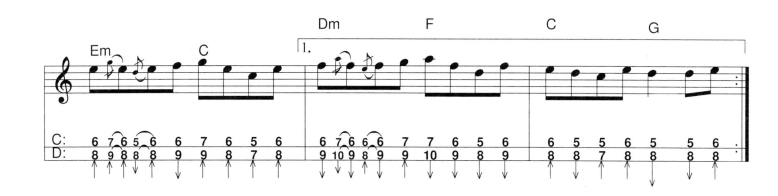

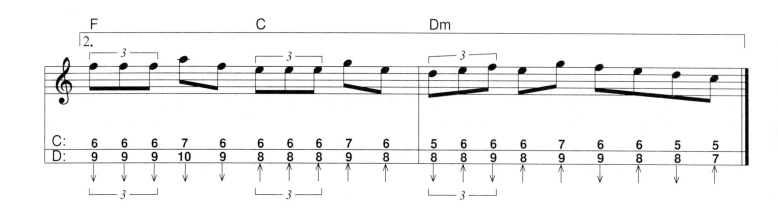

The Spanish Lady

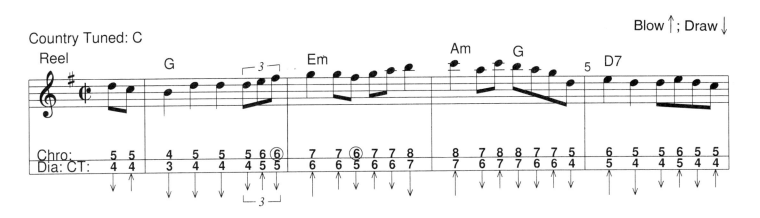

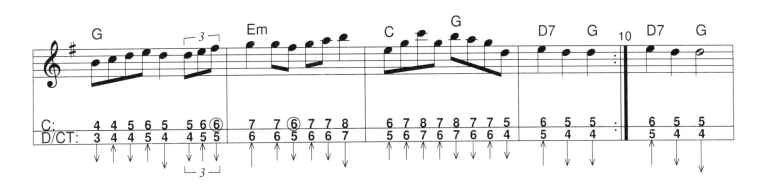

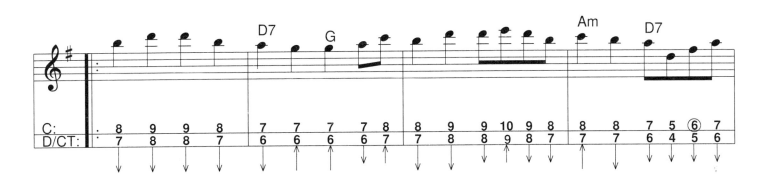

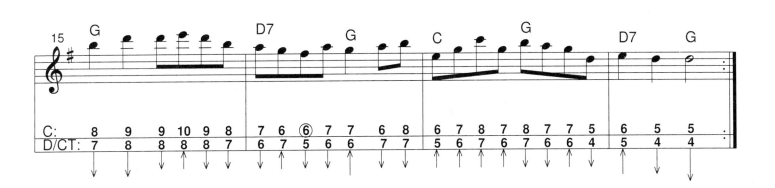

The Swallow's Tail

Swinging on the Gate

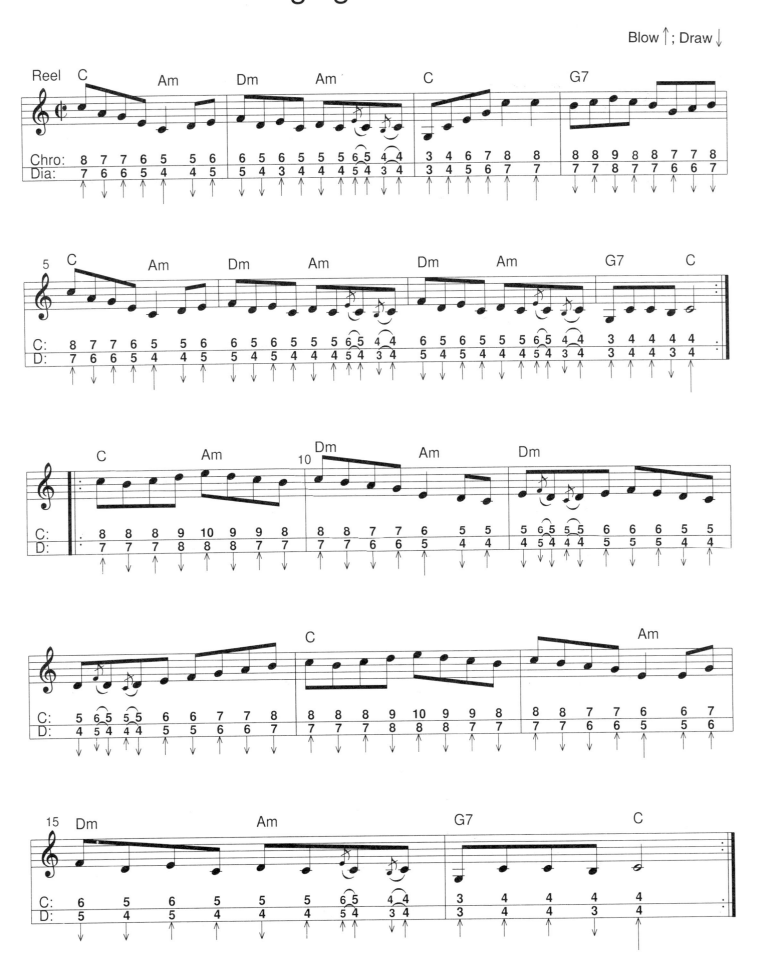

The Wexford Lasses

The Wind That Shakes The Barley

Blow ↑; Draw ↓

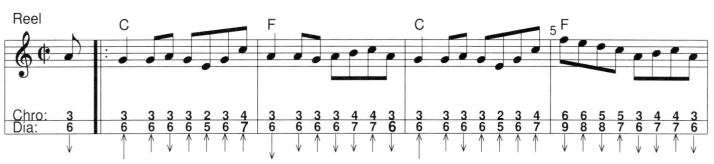

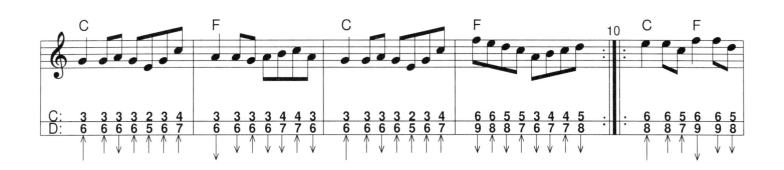

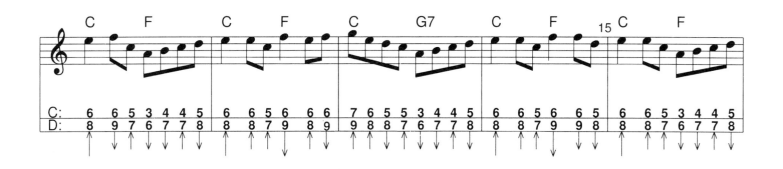

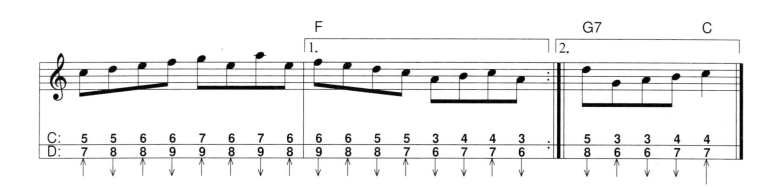

Alexander's Hornpipe

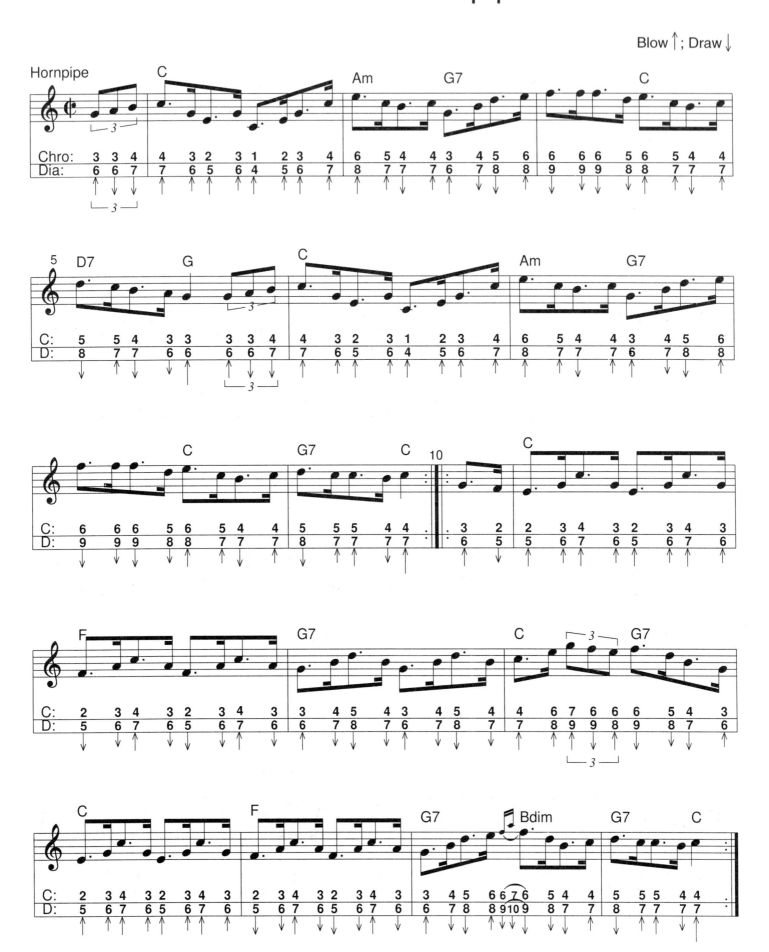

Back Of The Haggard

Blow ↑ ; Draw ↓

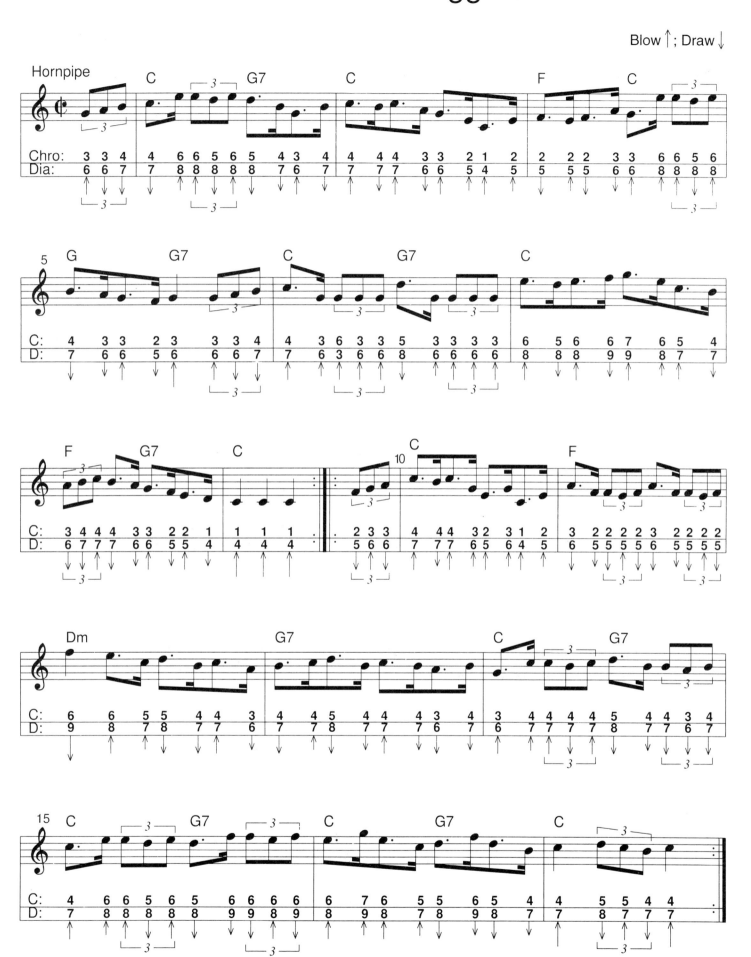

The Banks Of The Nile

The Boys Of Bluehill (O'Neill)

The Boys Of Blue Hill (2nd Tune)

Blow ↑; Draw ↓

Bryne's Hornpipe

Tommy Hill's Favorite

Blow ↑ ; Draw ↓

Cronin's Rambles

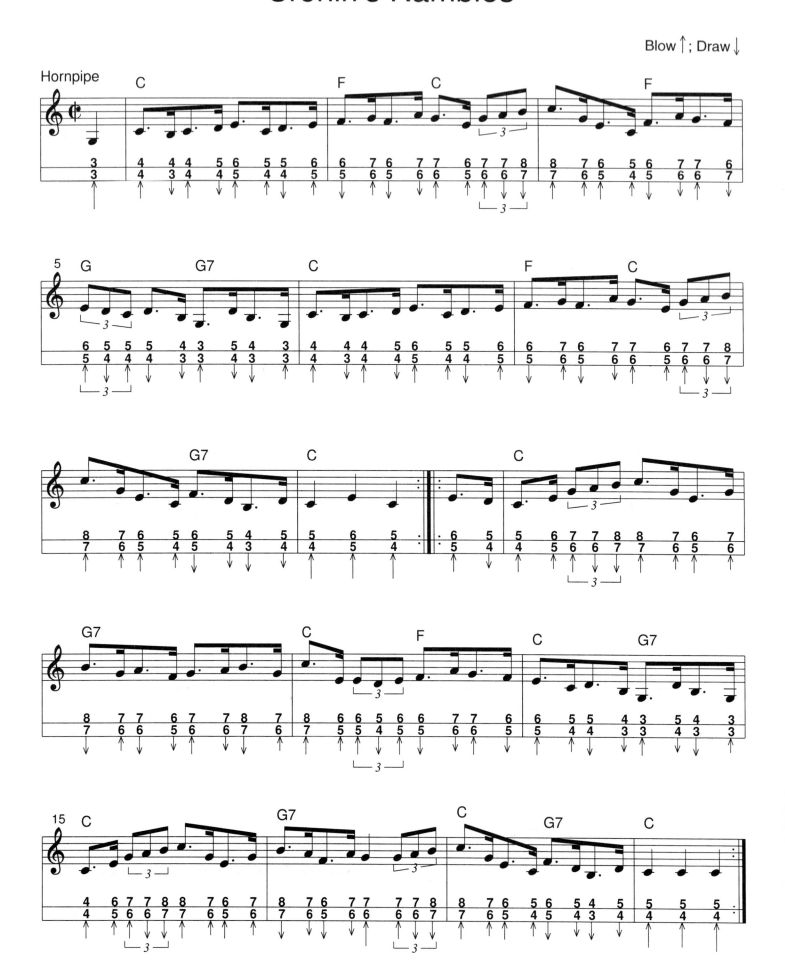

The Cuckoo's Nest

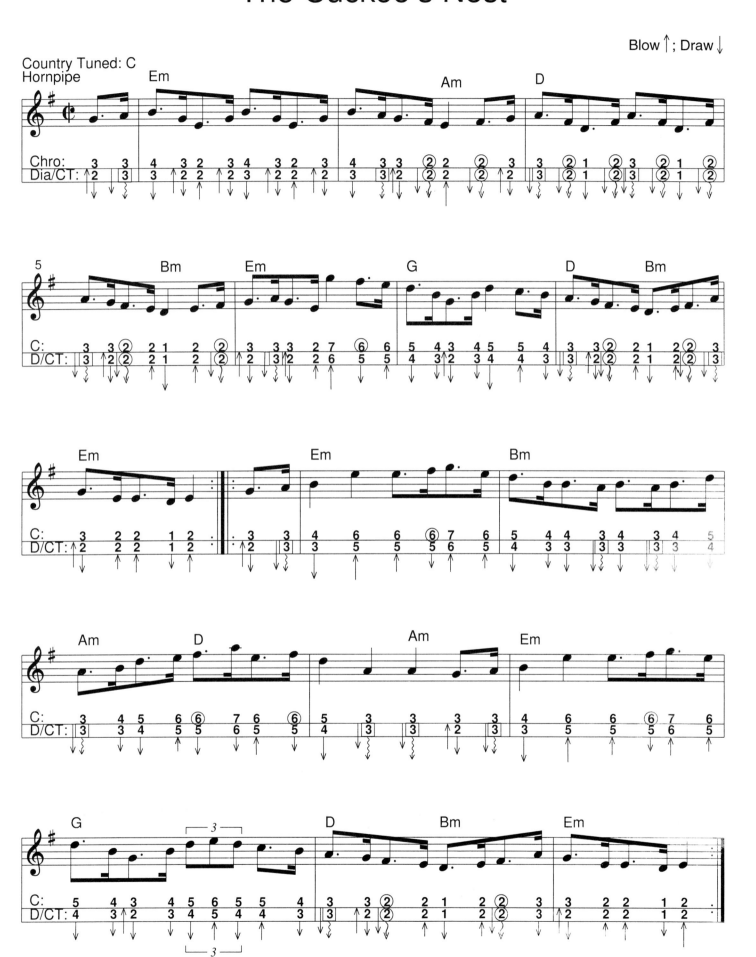

Drowsy Maggie

Blow ↑ ; Draw ↓

C Harp

Reel

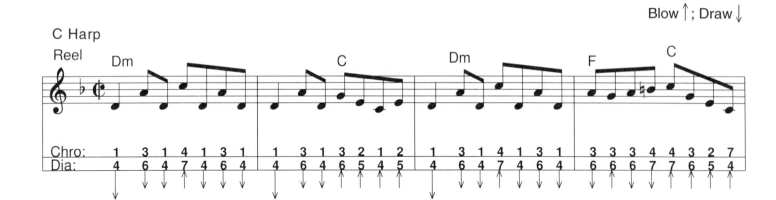

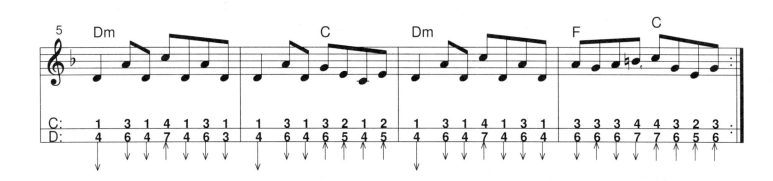

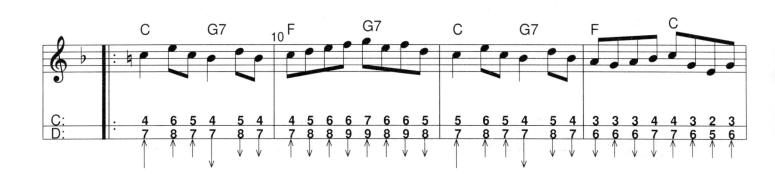

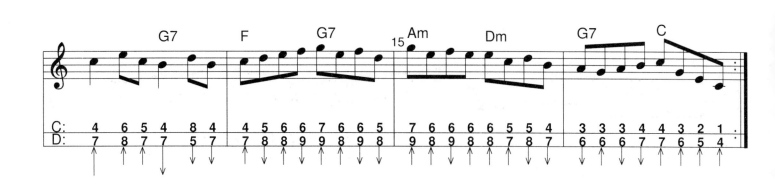

Dunphy's Hornpipe

Blow ↑ ; Draw ↓

Country Tuned: C

Hornpipe

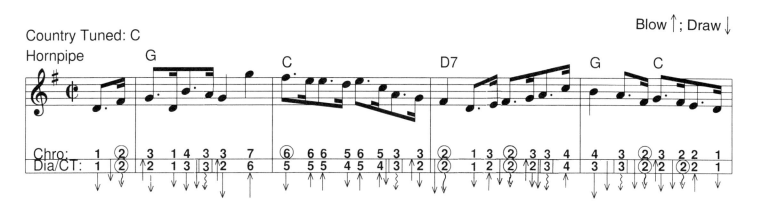

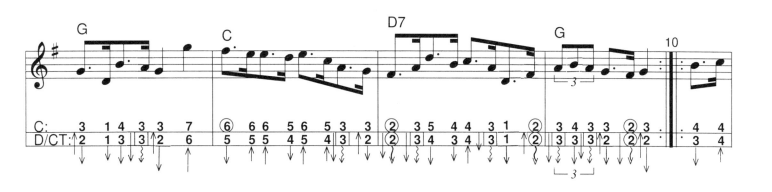

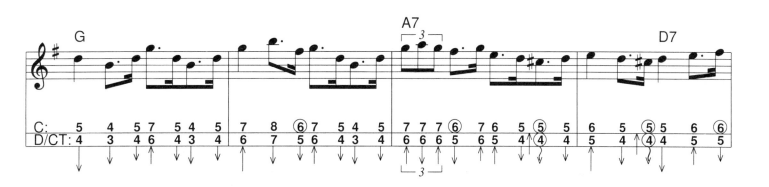

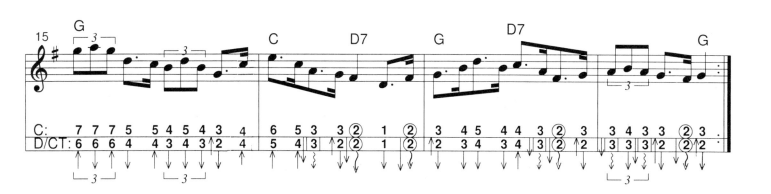

Durang's Hornpipe

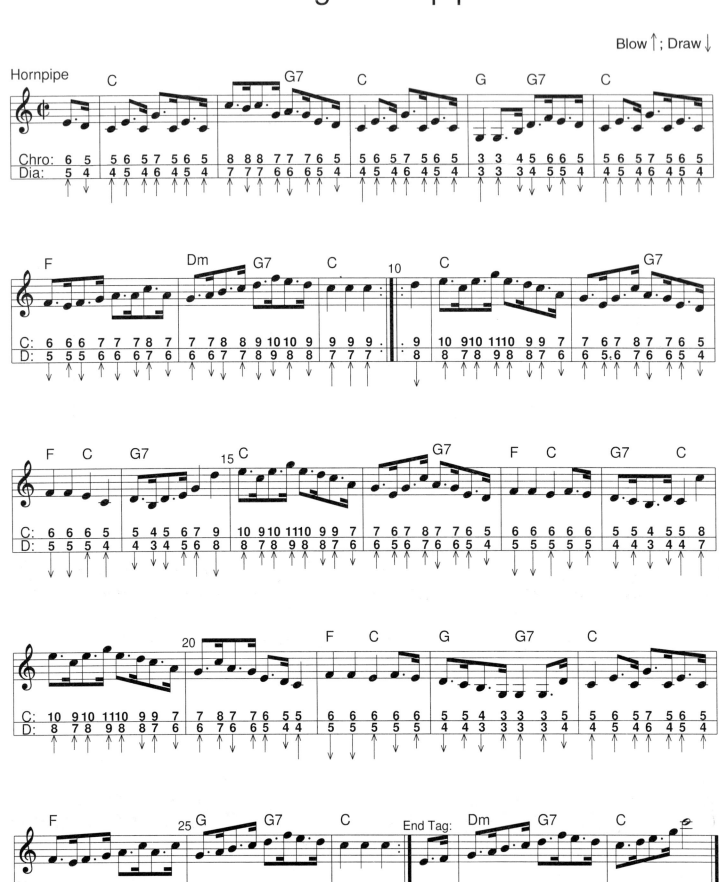

Father Dollard's Hornpipe

117

Fisher's Hornpipe

Blow ↑ ; Draw ↓

The Flowers Of Edinburgh

119

The Flowers Of The Flock

Blow ↑ ; Draw ↓

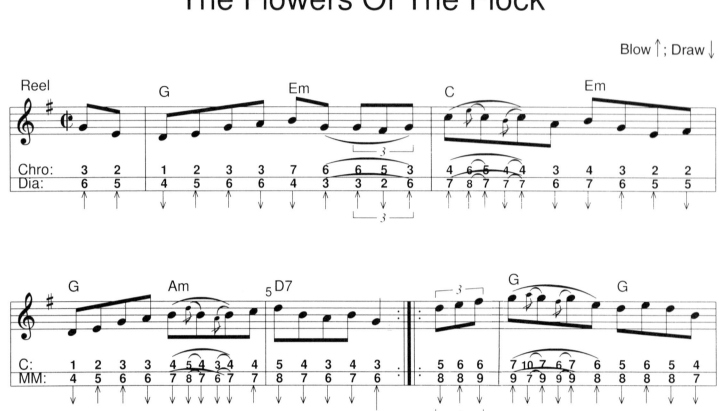

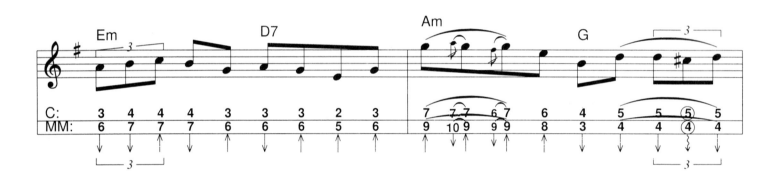

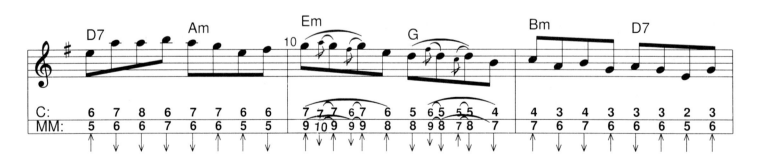

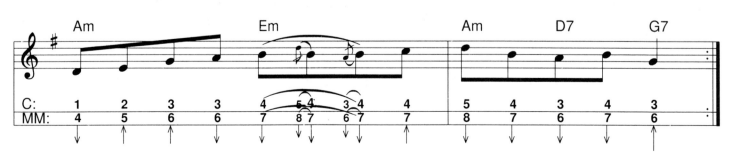

The Galway Hornpipe

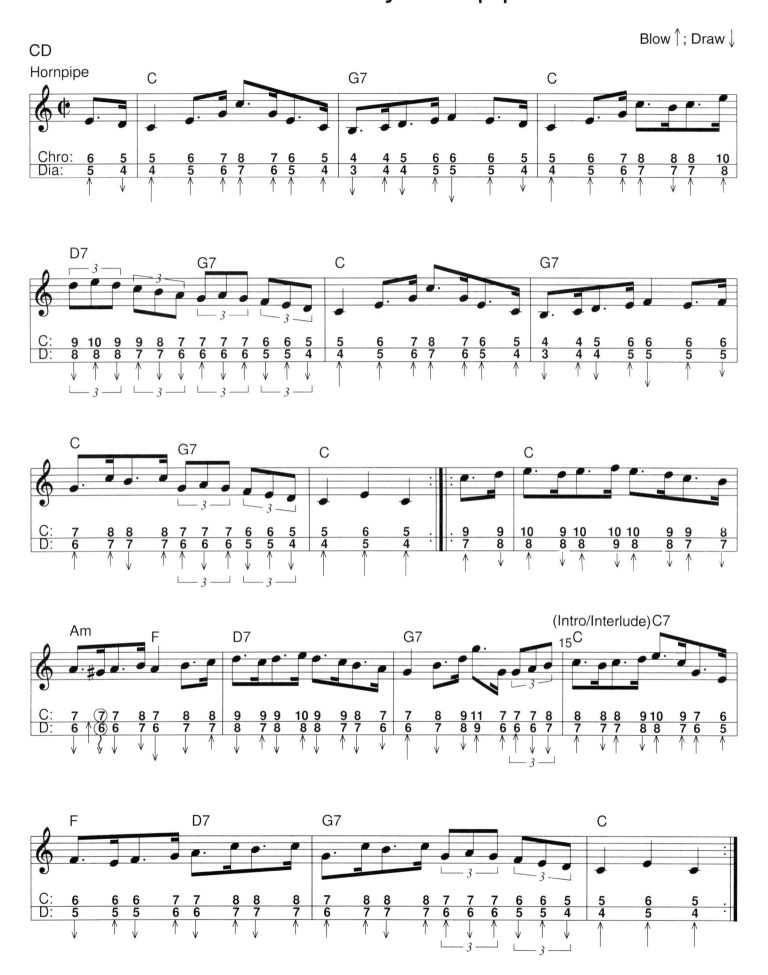

121

The Greencastle

Blow ↑ ; Draw ↓

The Harvest Home

Blow ↑ ; Draw ↓

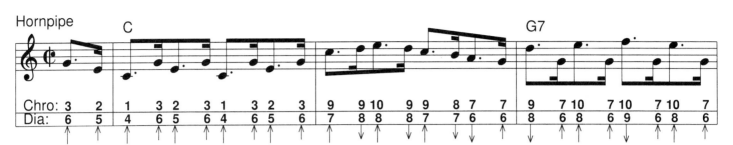

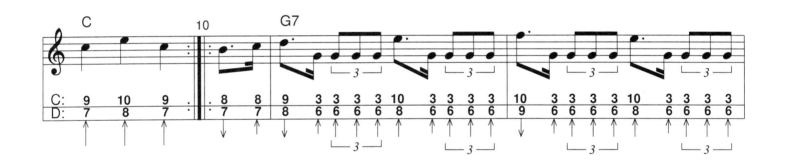

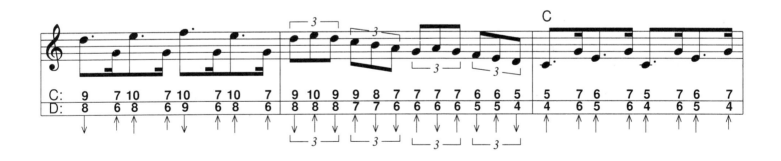

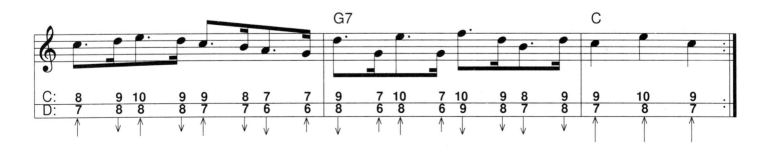

123

Julia's Wedding

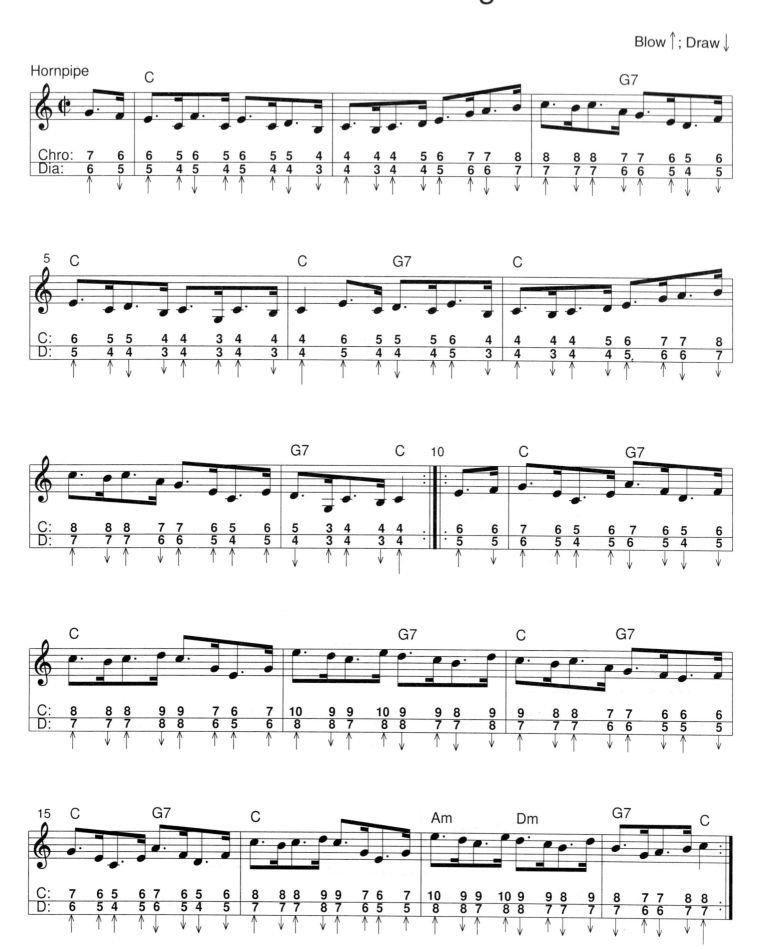

124

The Kildare Fancy

The Londonderry Hornpipe

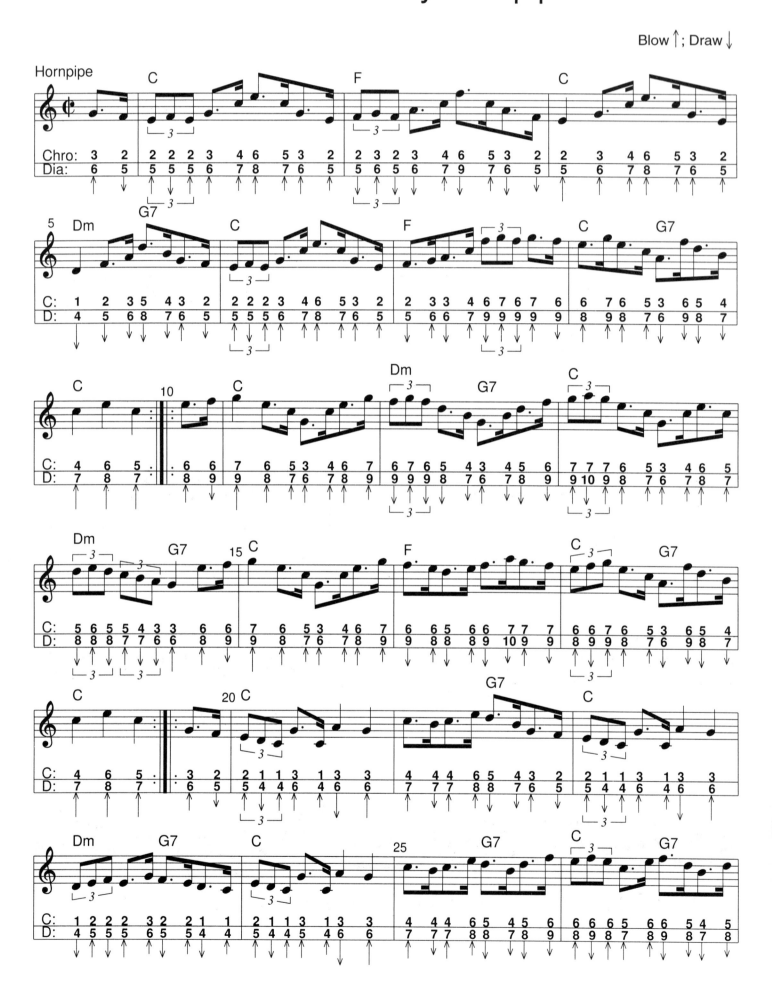

The Liverpool Hornpipe

Blow ↑; Draw ↓

Murphy's Hornpipe

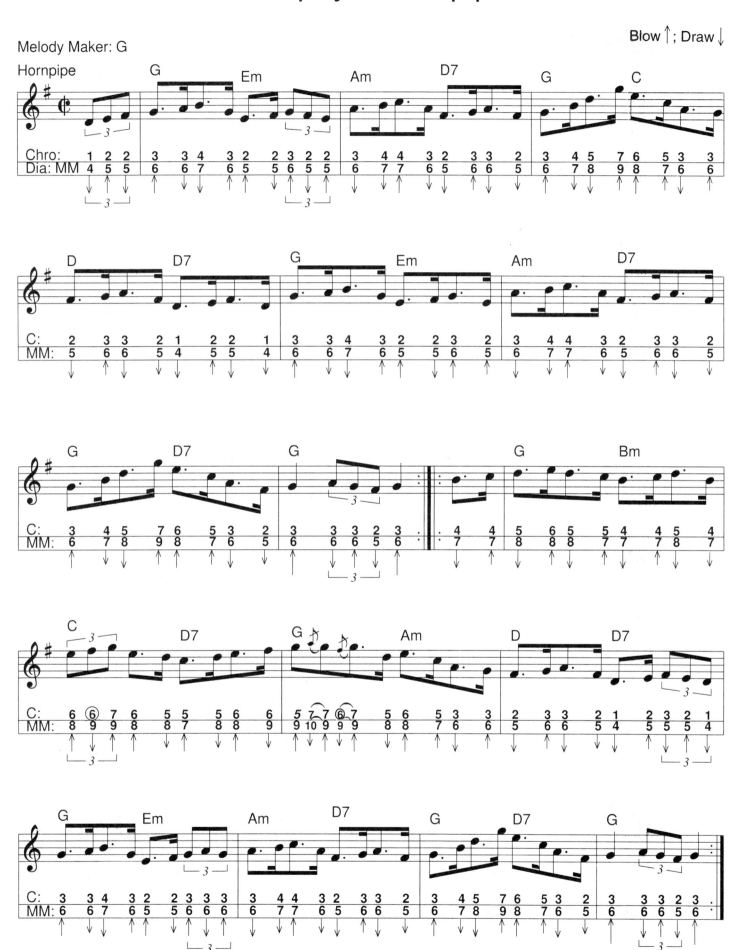

Off To California

The Pleasures Of Hope

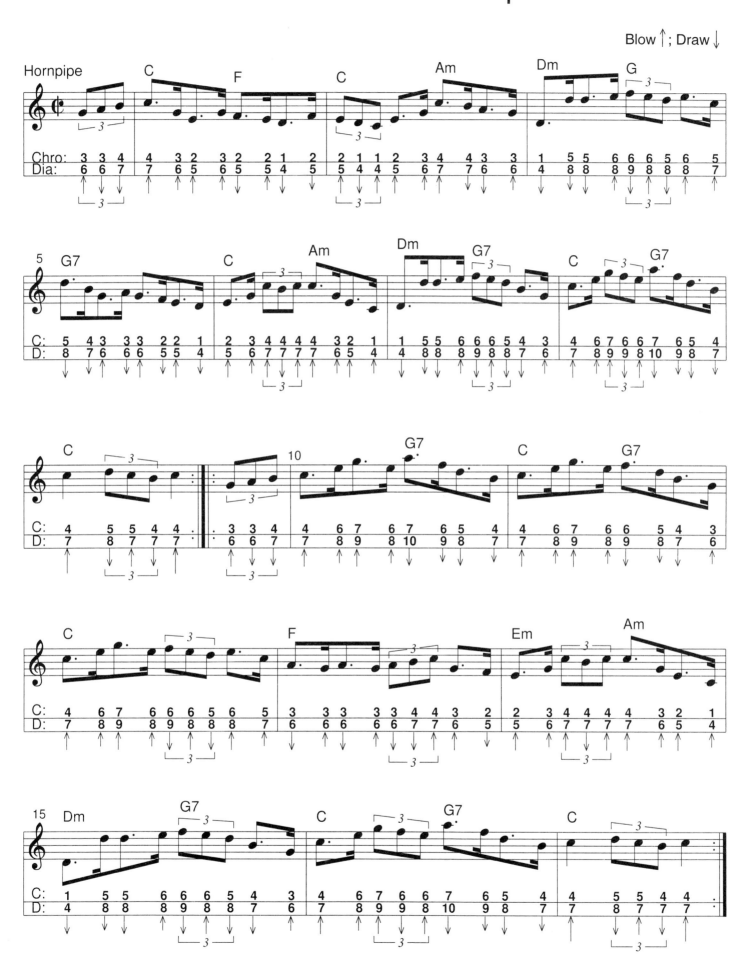

The Redhaired Boy

Rickett's Hornpipe

(Sailor's Hornpipe, 2nd Setting)

Blow ↑ ; Draw ↓

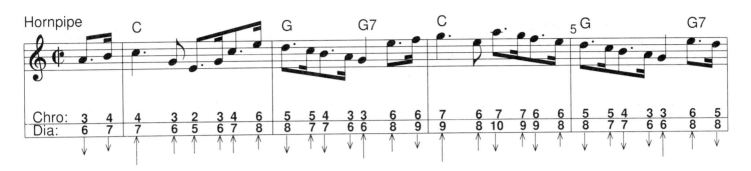

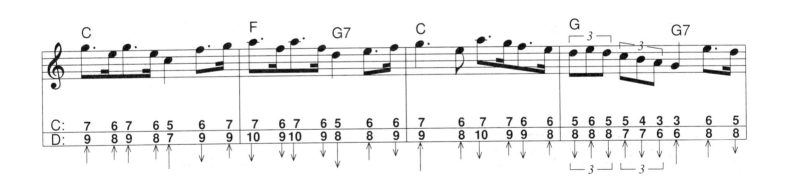

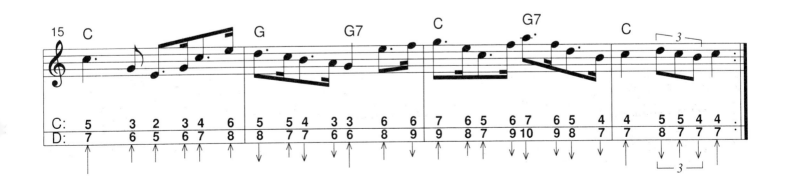

The Sailor's Hornpipe
(Original)

The Sailor's Hornpipe

(Popular Version)

Blow ↑; Draw ↓

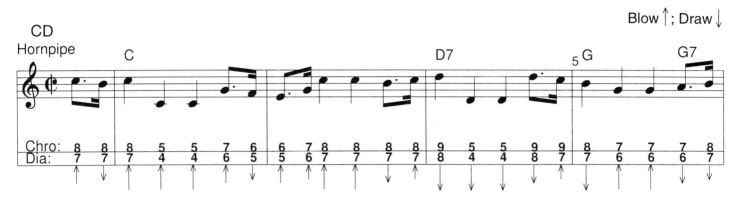

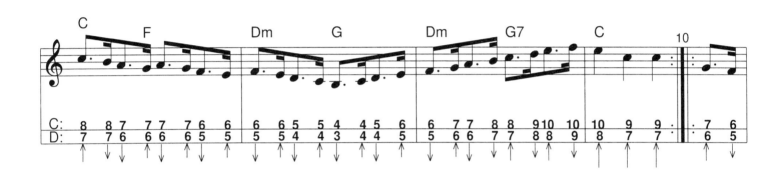

(Intro/Interlude)

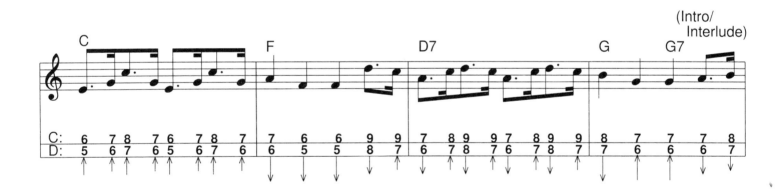

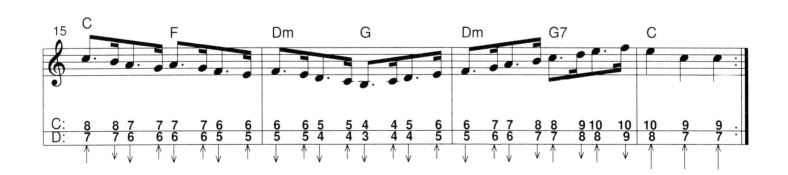

135

Soldier's Joy

Blow ↑ ; Draw ↓

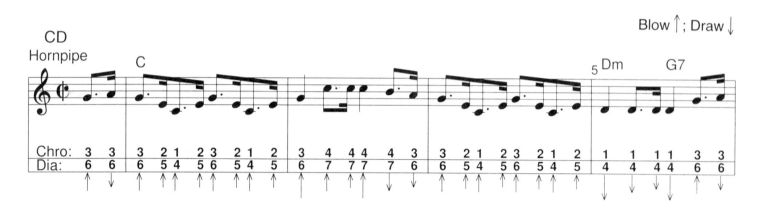

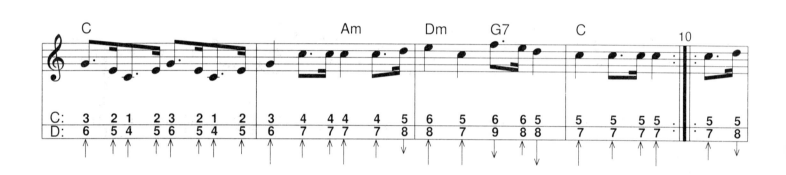

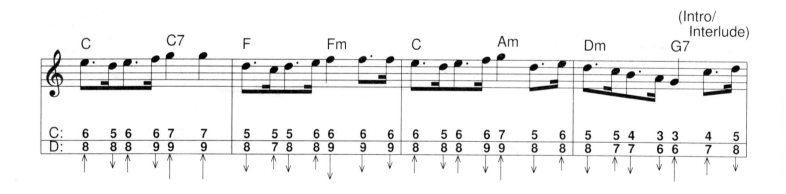

(Intro/
Interlude)

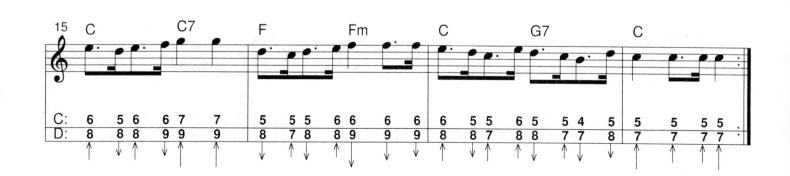

The Stack Of Barley

Blow ↑; Draw ↓

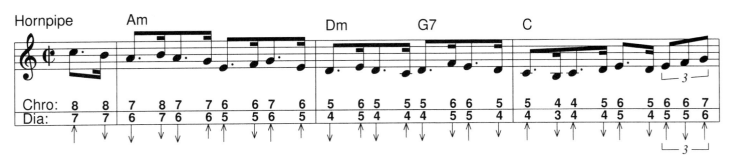

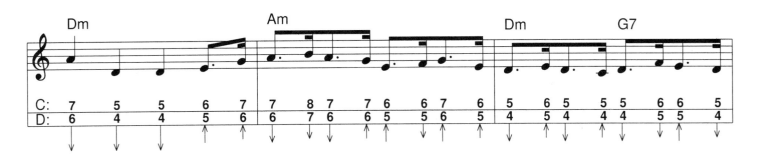

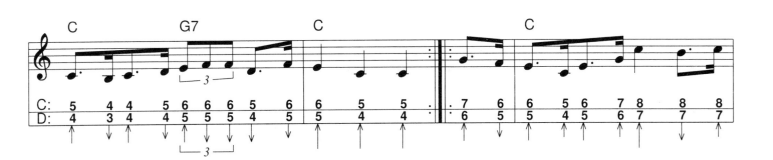

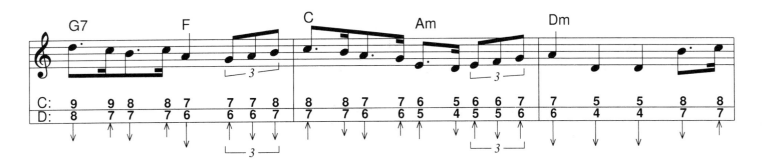

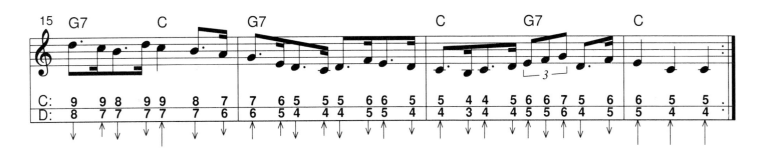

137

The Bold Deserter

The Lodge Road

Blow ↑; Draw ↓

Set Dance

139

The Garden Of Daisies

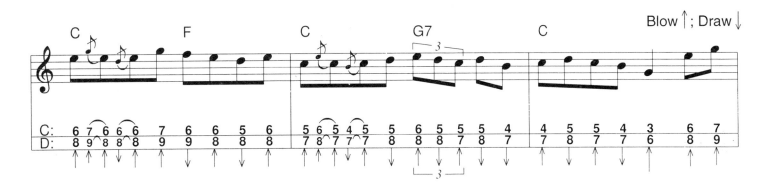

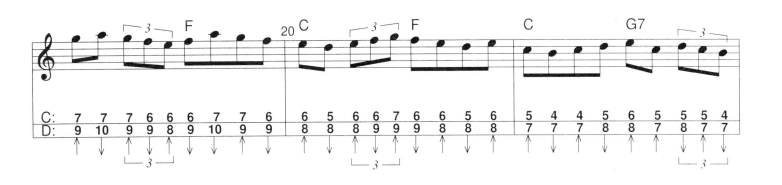

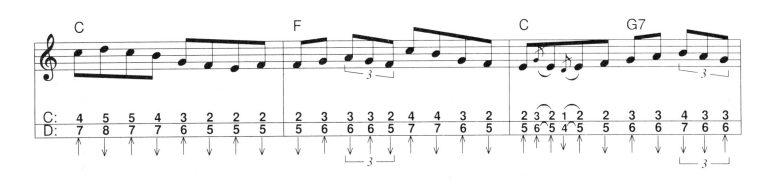

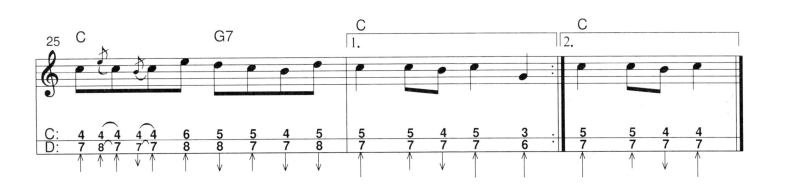

141

Blind Mary

Blow ↑ ; Draw ↓

O' Carolan

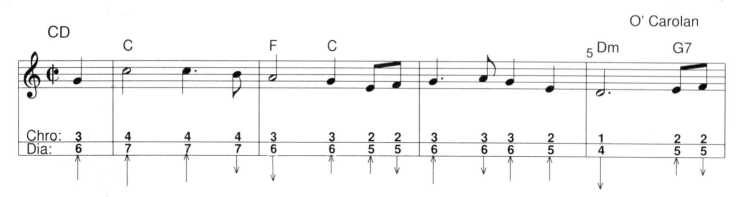

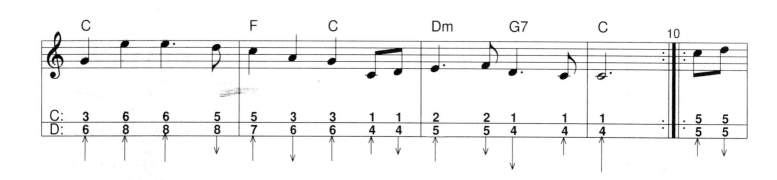

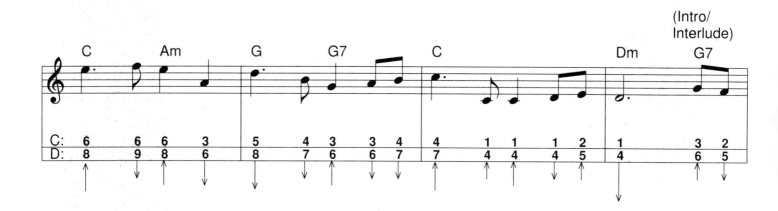

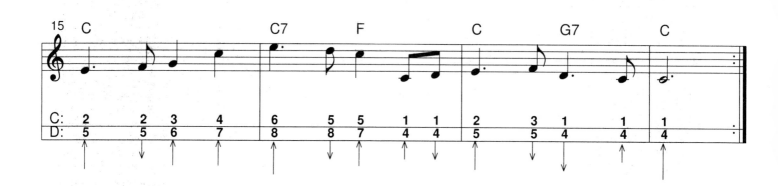

Miss Murphy

Blow ↑ ; Draw ↓

O' Carolan

Lord Inchquin

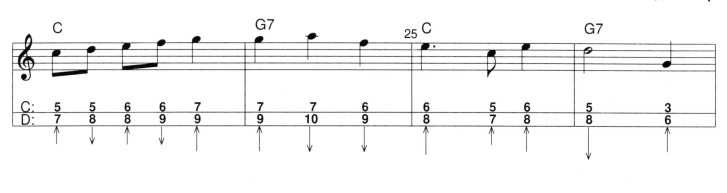

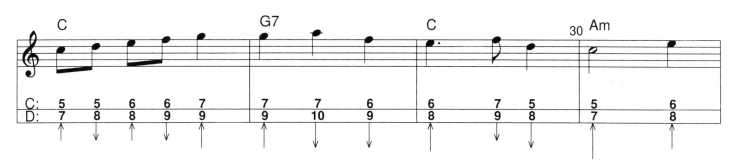

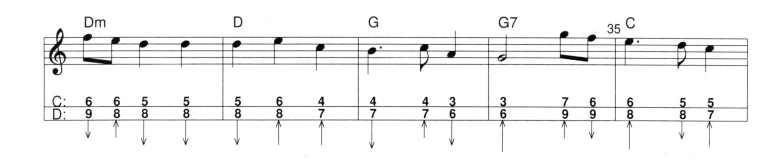

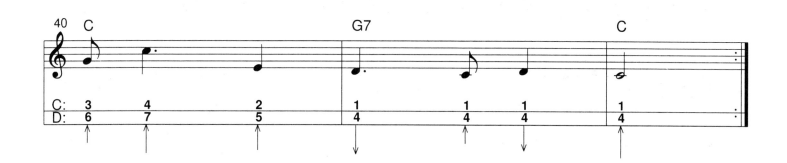

O' Carolan's Concerto

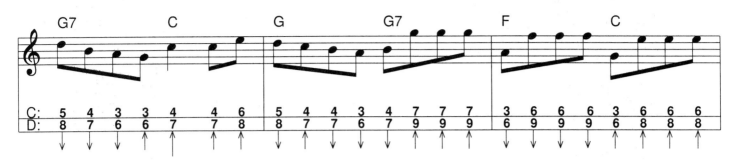

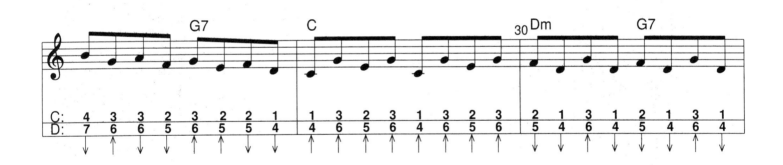

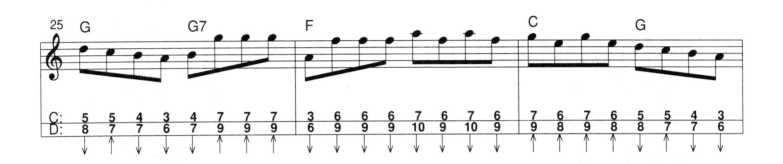

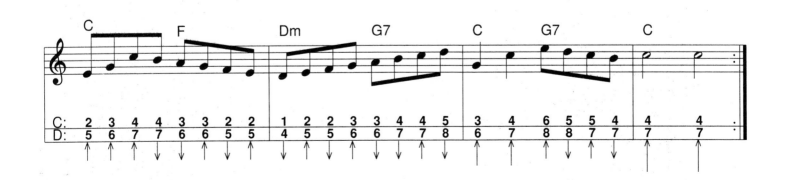

Planxty Denis O' Conor

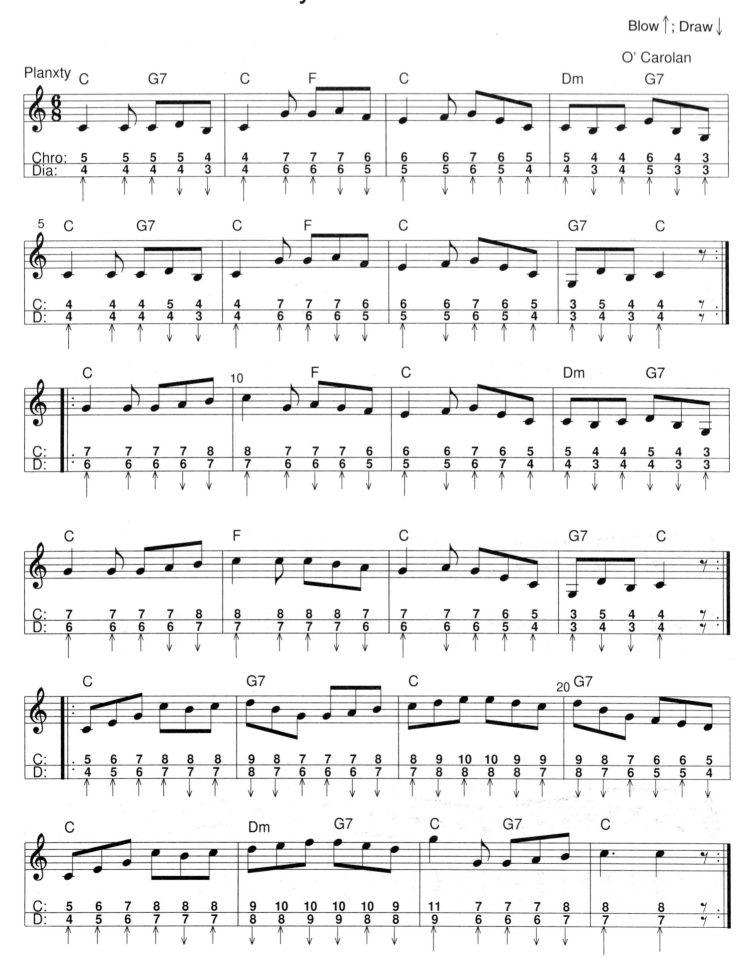

Planxty George Brabazon

Blow ↑ ; Draw ↓

Planxty Irwin

6/8 time

Blow ↑; Draw ↓

O' Carolan

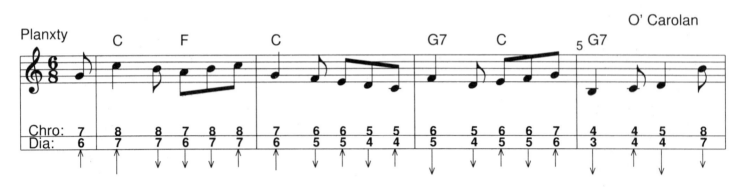

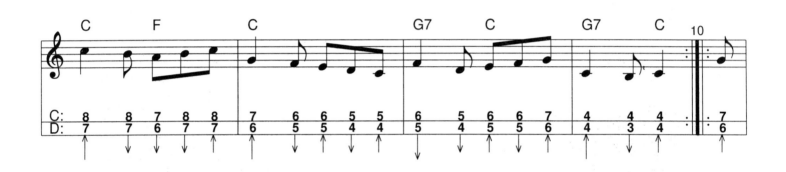

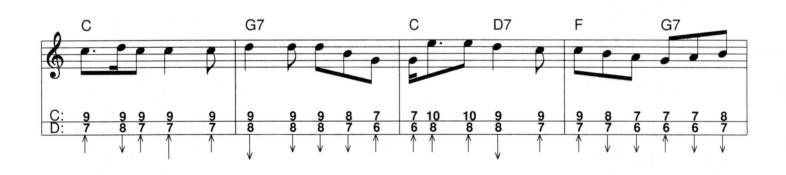

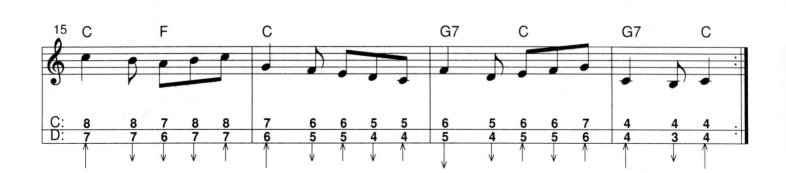

Planxty Irwin

3/4 time

Blow ↑; Draw ↓

O' Carolan

Sheebeg Sheemore